The Project Society

Anders Fogh Jensen

THE PROJECT SOCIETY

Translation: Sten Moslund

Aarhus University Press |

The Project Society

© The author and Aarhus University Press 2012

Graphic design: Jørgen Sparre

Cover photo: Lars Bahl

Printed at Narayana Press

Printed in Denmark 2012

ISBN 978 87 7934 722 9

Distributed by:

Aarhus University Press

Langelandsgade 177

8200 Århus N

Denmark

www.unipress.dk

Gazelle Book Services Ltd.

White Cross Mills

Hightown, Lancaster, LA1 4XS

United Kingdom

www.gazellebookservices.co.uk

ISD

70 Enterprise Drive

Bristol, CT 06010

USA

www.isdistribution.com

Indhold

The Project Society is a translation of my book in Danish, *Projekt-mennesket. Projektmennesket*, and this translation accordingly, is a rewriting of the main points of a far more comprehensive book, *Projektsamfundet* (2009). Some of the arguments and analyses and all of the references of the latter have been left out in this edition in order to equip the busy individual of the project society with a chance of acquiring the ideas of the book and to recognise themselves. If you are eager for more, I refer you to this book's big sister.

Copenhagen, November 2011
Anders Fogh Jensen
www.filosoffen.dk

I.

Everyone Has a Project

Everyone has a project. People have projects on behalf of them-selves and on behalf of others; they have their own projects and they have collective projects. We do projects at school and we carry out projects at work. Add to that all our spare time projects, and how it is sometimes hard to tell work projects from spare time projects. Projects cut across.

People have always had projects. Caesar had projects, Napo-leon had projects. Columbus also had a project. The difference is that today everyone speaks about their projects. They speak of everything they do as projects. "So, what is your project?" we ask our dinner partners. We used to ask people where they worked, if they had any children and how they spent their spare time.

Why does everyone speak in terms of projects? There is no doubt that it has a far more heroic sound to it to have a pro-ject than to have tasks to do or orders to fill. Projects express a kind of will or determination, something directed to the future, and something that exudes creativity. You are in the middle of doing something that will one day make good.

What is a project, then? It is something someone launches. Something someone is up to with someone else, with a cer-tain aim in mind. Actually 'project' means to throw something forward – something that is issued in a jet: pro-jacere. When Galileo spoke of the law of falling bodies, he spoke of pro-jectae, thrown objects in free fall. Someone who has a project has made a throw forward. So, a project is something that we do now with an aim to the future.

A project involves an activity which in most cases takes place in interaction with others. The rules, execution or aims of this activity are not laid down in advance; they are defined and elaborated as the project develops. In addition the project incarnates a spirit of shaping the future. The project is sustained by its activity – it works like pedalling a dynamo lamp: the project exists as long as activity is induced into it. When shut down, the project may be turned on again in different places only if you are doing something active with it or communicating with someone about it. It does not run all by itself: no building has ever erected itself nor has any thesis ever written itself just because time was passing.

The Danish playwright Ludvig Holberg spoke of *projekt-magere* –'project-makers' – already in 1724 in his play *Ulysses von Itaca*. A 'project-maker' was someone who went about conceiving ideas all the time which always came to nothing. At that time '*projektmager*' was a derogatory term, corresponding to the English term 'crank'. This is not the case anymore. In the mid-nineteenth century the Danish philosopher Søren Kierkegaard delineated the 'project-maker' or the crank as someone who is too preoccupied with possibilities to be able to see any necessities. According to Kierkegaard, man is a compound of possibility and necessity and the task of becoming a successful human being is about causing the compound to balance, or to form a 'synthesis' as Kierkegaard put it. One has to balance life's possibilities and necessities in a way that makes it possible for one to see that certain circumstances are necessary while retaining the ability to see that something else is actually possible. That it is possible to do something else. In a sense the kind of person who is capable of seeing only necessities is just as unfree as the kind of person who is incapable of seeing any necessities at all and constantly issues new projects without ever completing any. The former does not have the power to bend the world. The latter does not have the power to bend him-/herself. This way of being human holds a certain danger of living one's life inauthentically. Kierkegaard refers to such inauthentic living as 'despair'. In Kierkegaard, Holberg's 'projectmaker' is the kind of person who is driven to despair by the possible. When you are at a party with a person like that, he or she will keep talking about the next party.

In 1927 the German philosopher Martin Heidegger identified man as a being that constantly relates to the future. It has been claimed that man lives in the present, Heidegger said. But actually living in the present is essentially to be constantly oriented towards the future. When I am cooking I think ahead: I want to slice tomatoes so I have to find a knife. The mere fact that I started cooking at all was because I intended to eat. To be human means to be set on the future at all times.

In 1943 this caused the French existentialist Jean-Paul Sartre to define man as a being who has projects. To Sartre man is characterised as a being that is capable of denying the present. The power of imagination is an absolutely decisive quality of being human. To imagine, to envision, is to deny what is present now in order to be able to see something else. It is a matter of rejecting something in order to project something else. I want to go to Palermo, I envision myself in Palermo, i.e. my imagination rejects the actual: that I am here, in Copenhagen. What Sartre meant when he said that man is condemned to freedom was that he or she cannot but live in the future, as a being who envisions the future, who projects ideas into the future.

If Sartre is right there is nothing surprising about people always speaking about projects. Rather, it is surprising that they have not always done so. Indeed, people have always had projects, but to have projects has not always been crucial to the definition of what it means to be human. I believe that Sartre – apart from being good at describing the human condition – was also about to capture something that was in the offing at his time: that people were beginning to define themselves through their projects.

Already half a century before that, Friedrich Nietzsche had defined man as the animal that was yet to be determined. Until then philosophers had busied themselves for millennia with definitions of what man was supposed to be. Nietzsche's definition of man is closely connected with what is often referred to as the death of God: what happens when we no longer see ourselves as God's creation? Well, then it is up to us to create ourselves. How are we supposed to create ourselves? Through projects, Sartre replied.

I think that if we content ourselves with noting that now everyone is speaking about projects and that today everyone has projects, and that is just the way it is, we will fail to see an important connection between what it means to be human, on the one hand, and the way our societies have been shaped historically on the other. For in all this ado about projects there is a key to understanding how the universal raw material of being human is shaped by our time. I think that this 'homo projectus' is a being that has come about. Not because people have not had projects before but because the issue of having projects has never before been a pivotal point in society, has never before been the defining feature of an age. Likewise we would miss a useful conceptual key if we take it that people have always had projects. The first notion (now everyone speaks about projects) is a sociological notion, the other (people have always had projects) is an anthropological one. As a contrast to these – pardon me – superficial theses, 'so now we have projects' and 'man has always had projects', I would like to put forward the following thesis: our way of being human in the world is shaped by our time, our society being a society that organises itself through projects.

For many years philosophers have described what it means to be human – in fact, what it means to exist at all – by speaking of our dealings with some absolutely fundamental dimensions:

space, time, actions and relations. In trying to understand what it means to be human now it is useful to carry on this long-established tradition by asking: how are activities and people organised in our epoch, in our society? Which formations of life conditions are people offered and asked to deal with? My attempt at answering such questions has caused me to believe that 'the project' is a basic figure of organisation in our society and that it is decisive for the ways in which we unfurl space, time, actions and establish relations. In other words, my intention in the following is to describe the project society in order that we may get to understand what it is like to live in the project society, to be a projecting human being.

The project society did not appear out of nowhere. It is something that has slowly been developing in the course of the twentieth century. When defining man as a being who has projects, Sartre put into words something that was happening at his time. Twenty-five years later a revolt broke out: the revolt of '68, named after the student revolt in Paris that year. In reality a far more wide-ranging showdown with traditions and hierarchies was at stake. Now, much later, the current experimentations with alternative ways of living may seem like pubescent revolts against the order of a father figure or a mother's cleanly home. But what is really at issue is a protracted rebellion against certain ways of organising and governing people, a protest that stretches from the early sixties to the late seventies.

Then everything suddenly fell silent in the 1980s. What happened? Apparently the revolt had failed. Everyone moved back into families, got a car and a dog, and a steady job. True, there was a little bit of punk and squatter movements but most of all they looked like someone who were late by half a generation.

My first claim is that society and our ways of living have actually been changed by the revolt of the sixties, but what was tossed up into the air by the long revolt did not land as expected. In that respect I also make the claim that the revolt was not as spontaneous and independent as it sometimes pretended to be, that it was the continuation of a far longer movement, voiced by Nietzsche, Heidegger, Sartre, among others, and a number of writers like Virginia Woolf, Franz Kafka and Robert Musil.

My second claim is that that which was tossed up into the air landed again in the form of a project. Everything became quiet in the 1980s not because the showdown with the system and the forces of order had failed, but because the calls of the showdown for the breakdown of hierarchies, flat structures, human interaction and methods of working resulted in the project society.

If I am right that the showdown with earlier structures would later take the form of the project, it is no coincidence that everyone has projects and speaks about projects today. Or at least: this is an order that has been produced by history. Today the project is the very focal point of man, society and history. This leads me to a third claim: that the projectual organisation goes far deeper than being something that one simply has to say all the time, at work, in schools and in the civil service, it is a way of living. A way of being present in space and time. A way of making connections. A way of doing things. A way of living that we have not invented ourselves but have been dealt into our hands, that we have taken over and that we are now administering. The project society is not something we may choose, it is something that overarches us and is within us. It is something that is everywhere. When in a moment I set to examine what the project society consists in, I do so in order to understand contemporary man and his or her conditions.

By speaking of society as a project society I do not mean to say that all of society is organised by projects – nor do I mean that society is a project. What I mean is that the project as a certain way of unfurling space and time, of establishing relations and carrying out activities is becoming increasingly prevalent. Needless to say, there are other forms of organisation than that of the project, but as the project gains ground it relates to these earlier forms of organisation. In order for a project to be cross-disciplinary, for instance, there has to be specialist traditions with methods, practices and truths that the project may cross. The project constantly plays against or along with other ways of organisation – or disciplines. A cross-disciplinary project presupposes disciplines. Another example is the project of terror. Terror projects are organised in networks, which makes it difficult for conventional armies, organised by discipline in a pyramid shape, to counter the project. Projectual organisation challenges other forms of organisation, and as it does not reign supreme it constantly interplays with them. Hence, it is not only a true claim that I make when I say that the revolt landed as a project, which gave us the project society, it is also a claim that becomes truer day by day.

The project is not a form that just grew from one place, as for instance the project-organised firm. The rearrangement of our dealings with fundamental human conditions (time, space, actions, relations) may be explained as the transition to a project-organised society. As I will explain in more detail later, this is primarily a matter of transition from a disciplinarily organised society. New problems, solutions and possibilities arise in the project society, which pertain to the way in which we organise ourselves. These new ways of being may be experienced very differently within different areas, like football, dancing, the education of children, the construction of buildings, work, hospital service or warfare, even if rearrangements take place in more or less the same way. Yet there are basic features that are shared by all rearrangements which make it possible for us to speak of an overall transition to the project society.

To demonstrate how the project society works I would like to begin in one of the corners that, to me, breeds experiences of these new projectual conditions in striking ways: the way we dance.

2.

This Is How Project People Dance

In the middle of the dance floor one may feel ill at ease. You are standing there and you don't know exactly who you are dancing with, but you know that you have to look as if this is cool. You have to extract energy from within yourself or pick up energy from the music that you are expressing. Above all you have to express something.

There are at least two ways of doing this: you may close your eyes and look as if an awful lot of pleasure is running through your body, or deep melancholy, or you may throw your arms and legs about as if you were a bodily manifestation of some radio host's torrent of speech.

Once this phenomenon was referred to as dancing 'in the modern way'. Now it is just dancing. What remains the same is that everybody knows the way in which this dance works without following any hard-won dancing school system. You could say that we are all dancing in the same style – an energy style – in each our own fashion. Part of this style resides in the expression of energy and emotion. But the movements appear to be spontaneous, at least from the perspective of old ways of dancing. From that perspective the dance floor looks entirely chaotic.

It is my claim that the situation on the dance floor reflects the condition of our time. The dance floor is part of society and is structured in the same way – and if we take a closer look at this way of dancing we will be able to learn something about our society. Correspondingly, if we take a look at a large number of other phenomena, we will discover a number of common features and describe them as our society. The ways in which we make companies, educate children, play football, treat clients, prevent diseases, play games, manage the money, find friends, boyfriends and girlfriends, go to war and dance all have a number of structural features in common. This book is about how we organise ourselves and which experiences this entails.

Let us return to the dance floor for a while in order to get a first impression of our society. At closer inspection the dance floor turns out not to be a pure chaos. A logic unfolds in which the question about who is dancing with whom is not necessarily a question about who are holding each other's hands or even who are standing close to each other. Rather, the question is about who is dancing in the same style, i.e. who are making similar movements, occasionally – but far from all the time – addressing each other. The fact that no one puts their arms around each other or holds each other's hands opens up an endless number of ceaseless co-ordinations: who is dancing with whom, how many people are dancing with each other, how close are people to each other, where and how do people start dancing with each other, when does the dance begin, when does it end and what is a dance in the first place? At a concert for example, there will be a sliding transition from a slight wriggling to actual dancing. At a private party dancing may start in the bar, in the corner or in the middle of the living room, and in this way the location of the dance floor may be said to be decided by the activity. One does not necessarily ask someone to dance, but moves into the dance and dances one's way towards someone. One may be dancing among others or dancing with one person only or one may be dancing alone. One does not follow any set program, one improvises or creates variations of one's basic movements, or one imitates others. One may worm one's way in to dance with someone or one may move a bit away from someone while still keeping contact. Or one may do both, gradually scaling down the dance with some people while moving in on someone else. There is a logic in this that decides who is dancing with whom without any programs being played. To a large degree this logic is sustained by *activity*, i.e. if one is dancing and with whom one is dancing is decided by the actual activity, and not by a program being played within a specific framework. Among other things, it is the fact that the dance is only kept going by the activity of individuals themselves that causes emotion to enter the dance: as dancers can no longer rely on any accustomed program being played, they have to project a keen activity that unfurls a dance rather than rehearses a dance.

Dancing has not always been like that. But it has changed before. From the fifteenth to the nineteenth century dancing comprised line dancing and circle dancing in which groups were dancing together according to specific patterns. At Court there were complicated figure dances in which four or eight people grouped around a central person or a central couple, usually the king or the king and the queen. There were also *processional dances* in which couples follow each other as we know it from e.g. 'Oh! Susanna'. In the country there were contra-dances or folk dances in which couples would lead the dance while the rest would copy. What these dances all have in common is that they are collective rehearsals of a programmed pattern.

In the nineteenth century codified couple dances emerged as we know them today: waltz, polonaise, mazurka, etc. They are what I choose to refer to as *disciplined* dances, i.e. individuals have been trained in a number of step sequences which determine a certain movement within a room at a certain time which the dancers may replicate with each other. Disciplined dancing, e.g. the waltz then entered into social situations in which dancing was part of the act of socialisation without this necessarily entailing any emotional implications or erotic undertones; it was etiquette.

Space was divided into zones (the dance floor and all the space outside the dance floor where people may ask each other to dance), and time was divided into pieces of music. One asked someone to dance outside the dancing zone, entered the dancing zone together and ran through the program for the duration of a certain number of numbers. The fixed rules of how the dance might unfold made it possible to dance without any implications of appraisal, games or negotiations – although the rules did not exclude this either.

In the beginning of the twentieth century, up until the 1920s, schools of dancing grew vigorously. They taught the children of the respectable citizens to replicate the programs (dances) that were an obligatory part of their social position.

With the Charleston in the 1920s the space between the dancers began to grow and grew further with the arrival of rock and roll and the Jitterbug in the 1950s. Dancing grew increasingly unrestrained as the distance between the partners grew.

In the course of the first two thirds of the twentieth century two things slowly began to happen: dancing partners increasingly began to stand on their heels, and the distance between them kept growing. The turning point was the arrival of the Twist in the 1960s: partners let go of each other. As they no longer held on to each other the necessity of coordination disappeared. Now the steps got so simple that nobody needed to attend dancing schools to practice them. Had it not been for the fashion waves in the wake of movies like *West Side Story* (1961), *Saturday Night Fever* (1978), *Fame* (1982-87) and *Flash Dance* (1983), the dancing schools would have been ruined.

Dancing at parties and night clubs is no longer sustained by a fixed scheme in space and time, by a program. It is sustained by individuals who keep throwing energy into their own movements. And it is possible to pick and choose one's way of doing it because there is no program to adhere to.

When something is released from its codification as an automatic pattern and becomes a matter of choice, this choice becomes a sign. You may have done something different, but now you made the choice of standing like that, to do like that, to look like that. The science of sign systems is called semiotics.

When the space between the partners in a dance is no longer determined from the outside by rules, but is decided from within the dance itself, this space becomes a sign. In other words: separating the partners introduces a semiotics of space. The basis of the theory may sound like this: the closer the more intimate. Yet, as I have said, the dance may easily be sustained at a distance as long as there is some form of contact or approximation of style of movement.

Secondly, the possibility of spatial distance introduces a semiotics of touch: does she want to hold hands or doesn't she? Does he want to coordinate movements or doesn't he?

Collective space is open to be negotiated whereby collectivity opens to negotiation during the dance. One may gradually move out of one collective space while entering another, or even choose to position oneself in-between two collectivities.

How is that so? Well, because the dance no longer takes place within a closed space as in a room. The dance is an open space on account of its activity. That is also why the location of the dance floor depends on activity and not on some location that was predetermined as a dancing space. Rather than speaking about space as a room or box or stage, in which or on which actions take place, we have to imagine a space that is kept in a state of extension by activity when speaking of the project society. Of course all the dancing and all other projects take place in a three-dimensional space, but this space is not decisive for the dance. In relation to three-dimensional spaces it may be said that the activity of dancing extends a plane between the dancers. The project is a pocket of activity within a network in which people do something together or on their own.

The same applies to the question of time. The duration of the dance is not predetermined by a certain number of tracks during which a particular pattern of movement is to be replicated. The dance lasts as long as there are movements and it stops whenever the movements die out. Hence, individuals have to keep throwing energy into the dance in order to keep it going. And that is why bad tracks are so deadly to the dance: since it is not possible to fall back on a reiterable program or sequence, but one has to keep throwing emotion and energy into the dance, a bad track is something that makes the dynamo lamp of the project very tough to pedal. That is why one may justly leave the dance if a bad track comes up. The reason why time is no longer stretched or staked out in advance is not because the DJ samples the transition from one track to another, rather this owes to the absence of formal rules. The rules of knowing the same steps, and the fact that they are infused with etiquette, stretches out time within a demarcated space of time. Now that this coordination has eroded, time is stretched out by activity. If anything, the sampling of tracks supports the fact that time too is brought up for discussion all of the time.

The individualisation of the activity within the dance, from the Twist and on, means that the possibility of dancing is also up to the individual. Opening up space and time for dancing is an individual matter. You may very well keep on dancing even if the one or the ones you are dancing with cease to dance, but it requires that you alone keep throwing your energy into the dance.

One of the many questions that crop up after the subversion of order, systems and hierarchies in the 1970s is how gender relations have come down. I suppose I am stating the obvious when I say that the impossibility of any clear answer to this question has caused a great deal of confusion on the dance floor on the subject of leading, and that the consequence is that partners have started to lead themselves and to follow each their own way of dancing. Without a doubt it is still possible to take the lead or to allow oneself to be led, but this involves roles that one may (not easily) enter into or out of. When the dancing schools of today are to teach the individuals of the project society how to dance, not only do they have to teach male partners how to take the lead, they also have to teach the female partners to let go of the lead.

One of the keys to success in the project society is connections. In the world of the old codified dance, males asked females to dance within a zone outside the dance floor, receiving a yes or a no, and if a male received a yes he would lead the female onto the dance floor and dance a number of dances with her. The initiative was there for males to take but they exposed themselves to the risk of a no. Females might receive a yes in the form of an invitation to dance, but there was no risk of a 'no, thank you!'. Women's 'no, thank you!' in the dancing schools and at dances and balls was silence.

The situation women were in then is the situation everyone is in today in the sense that connections are made on the dance floor. As no one is ever asking for a yes or a no anymore, no one refuses anyone's requests. And still not everyone is dancing with the ones they want. Why is that? The transition to the project society is a transition from a logic of no to a logic of yes: you may try to make an impression and if anybody else thinks it is interesting you may open a space of activity together. If not, you have already opened your own dancing space in the attempt.

I know that people are still asking each other to dance, but what I am getting at here is a logic that is becoming increasingly prevalent without being hegemonic. In order to make it easier to see the project society I present it in its pure form. As mentioned, in practice there are residues of earlier forms of organisation and distribution that the project society interacts with, and I will return to this in the following six chapters.

Just as we may exhibit ourselves in different projects, as for example by working for free as an intern to prove that one is suited for the company, we may also dance with friends and girlfriends. In order that anyone will attach themselves to you it is crucial that you are active and outgoing. The ones who hide are not making themselves attractive to projects. By contrast, it is possible to dance your way into the affections of someone who is already dancing.

One may then go on to ask what kind of movements – activities – are actually unfurling. Apart from a number of imitations of a range of movements from non-dancing activities, as for instance the air guitar, there are a great number of steps and twists and turns within the dancing which are not just emotional expressions but imitations of earlier dances and their composure and rhythmic.

The shattering of forms occurred within a large number of disciplines at the same time. The ways in which forms fall apart is experienced differently within different activities – in the lives of singles, in hospital services, social services, skate boarding, and so on – even if they occur in similar ways. It is the similarity of the transformations that make it possible for us to speak of an overall transition to the project society.

So far, on the basis of the model of dancing, we are able to say four things about the project society: firstly, the project society emanated from a showdown with an earlier order – a showdown that took place over a long time. The modern energy dance – which I refrain from calling a modern dance as modern dancing denotes what I would refer to as the traditional and disciplinary dances – the energy dance is, accordingly, the outcome of the programs of traditional dances being blown apart.

Secondly, it is not a chaos of dancing without any kind of logic, but activities that are ordered according to the principles described above. These principles are rarely peremptory, they are normal occurrences. No one has decided that this is the way it must be and then written down the rules. It is from the regularity produced by their commonness that one may distil their systematic. The practice of this systematic is what I refer to as the project society.

Thirdly, this is a systematic that cuts across a vast range of areas, as we shall see, and this has to do with the fact that our dealings with space, time, action and the formation of relations – i.e. the very basic elements of experience – has been going through a transformation; it may have been difficult to predict this transformation forty years ago, but I believe that it is now possible to see how it may be understood as a project society.

Finally, and fourthly, the project society grows out of the previous society and earlier experiences of space, time, action and relation. The project society always takes place through a discussion with, imitation or transgression of preceding for-mations and it is impossible to understand the project society without this. The old society – the age of programs, codes, schemes and square spaces – is what I will refer to with one word as the *disciplinary society*. To be able to understand what distinguishes the project, one has to understand the founda-tion on which it takes place – everyday repetitions, the main-tenance of the system, rules and justice and the reiteration of the program. For this reason I will direct a moment's attention to what the project society bases itself on, what it transgresses, dismantles and connects with.

3.

From Plan to Project

The project society is a society in which all activity is organised through projects. A project does not repeat itself, and for every new project you have to find out how to do things as you go along because you have never done the same thing before. I know very well that there are 'project manuals' in companies, prescribing what steps to take in a project. In some cases such 'projects' are assignments that have merely been renamed as projects – because projects seem far more spectacular and employees who work on projects appear more heroic – and in other cases they are something in-between projects and assignments. Usually an assignment or an obligation has a line of procedure, a fixed objective and a predetermined criterion of evaluation. Naturally, assignments and obligations are still around.

In the following I will draw an exaggerated image two kinds of society: a society that once was and still exists (the disciplinary society), and another type of society whose dominance keeps growing (the project society).

The project society is a form of organisation that becomes increasingly dominant as a manner in which one deals with the world, raises problems and suggests solutions. Accordingly, to say that we are living in a project society is only a qualified truth: we are living in a project society ever more so.

The other way round it also has to be acknowledged that projects have always been around. A king who wants to build a castle, a government that wants to build a bridge, a bank robber who wants to rob a bank. They were all projects. The project society is distinguished not by the fact that there are projects but by the fact that the project has become a central principle of organisation. And this is the principle that is increasingly winning through.

The centralisation of the project is part of a process of decentralisation. In a world organised by projects there is no central point from where one may take in the whole of society and adjust its parts. Such central points were not always to be found in what I call the disciplinary form of organisation, but at least this was an ideal. The ideal of the dance teacher was to get all the dance students to perform the same movements simultaneously, or it was an ideal that the work at each machine was carefully coordinated according to an overall plan. If one reads the literature of the past on organisation or textbooks of pedagogy, books on dancing, warfare or directions for fighting epidemics, one may see the disciplinary principle of central coordination at work: This is how we will structure space from a central position.

Between 1750 and 1850 society gradually transformed into a society organised through discipline. It is worth noticing that the society I am referring to as the disciplinary society thinks very much in terms of space, and that it understands the other three categories on the basis of the spatial: time is understood in spatial terms as a chain of events moving through space. Relations are understood as structures within a whole. Action is understood as movement through space.

Since discipline starts with an organisation of space, it also lays the foundation for an organisation of activities. The disciplinary way of approaching a problem is an attempt to architecturise one's way out of the problem: to allot the right place to things and to determine the kind of activity that is to take place in each place. Discipline works through fixation, and any movement is to take place from one fixed point to another. A place is allotted to each pupil, for instance, and no one is allowed to move during the lesson; a pupil may say something only when prompted. In this way a lesson may take place as an examination with the teacher as a central point, surveying the room. Next, there is a window in the classroom door for the principal as he moves down the hall surveying each class and each teacher the way each teacher surveys the pupils. Hence the same principle of control is repeated at different levels and is ideally drawn together at a central point.

Control is executed through the act of looking, which is why visibility is an important preparatory measure for control. However, in comparison with the project society this visibility is issued from a central quarter and not from the individual. The individual is observed by the system. This is turned upside down in the project society in the sense that the individual now has to make himself or herself visible. Here the danger is not getting caught in doing something wrong as much as it is not to be seen. Accordingly, it is not so often the fidgety boy who gets into trouble anymore as much as it is the quiet girl. In contrast, it is the concord between correct and ideal behaviour that is rewarded in the society organised by discipline – in physical education, orthography, drills and the instruction of all kinds of proficiencies.

Discipline is a form of rationalisation and organisation that divides society into compartments and sub-compartments. In societal terms such units are called institutions. Each institution is organised in the same way, it is self-enclosed, and within the individual institution the same organisation is repeated once again. The stores manager is the manager of the store just as he is an employee in relation to the upper management. A bureaucracy is another example of such hierarchical forms of organisation that prevail by sorting things, following rules and operating in hierarchies.

This type of society has many names depending on what one attaches the greatest importance to. Most commonly it is referred to as the modern, industrial or urban society. I have chosen to follow in the steps of the French philosopher Michel Foucault by emphasising its disciplinary features because I am particularly interested in the ways in which people organise themselves. But the space of the disciplinary society remains a modern, industrial and urban space. Work takes place at the workplace, cooking takes place in the home, sports on the sports ground, care of the children in the day care centres, etc. Movement is movement between institutions. Production is industrial and circulation is material. Maps are divided into countries with cities. Transport involves physical movement between these cities, if necessary across borders to cities in other countries.

In the project the disciplinary configuration of spaces is dismantled. As a smooth horizontal surface the project cuts across disciplinary spaces and institutions. The project needs to be cross-disciplinary, cross-institutional; in short, transversal.

For too long we have been much too ready to ascribe the growing number of disagreements between spaces and their functions to modern means of communication. We think that work started flowing into our homes, cafes into banks, the promotion of health into holidays and training into the workplaces because of the arrival of the computer, the mobile phone and the Internet. But we have failed to see how this development was also pushed forward by a simultaneous restructuring of forms of organisation. For a long time the development of the size of batteries, for instance, was lagging behind the development of the portable machines they were meant for – and when suddenly the size of batteries was reduced, making it possible to carry phones and computers, it may be more correct to see this as a result of a need arising alongside a restructuring of society where people now had to engage in cross-institutional activities and communication while moving around.

Institutions graft onto each other, not least through projects. As opposed to the disciplinary society, the project constitutes the kind of channel through which all that was differentiated by discipline is now hybridised. Something more fundamental than technological development is at stake, and even if technological development may have helped transforming the principles of social organisation, this does not explain the de-differentiation of institutions. Calling and writing each other across institutions had been possible for a long time, but institutions were not mixed because communication took place within the disciplinary divisions.

The disintegration of spatial boundaries caused by the project is not all that happens though. Projects are launched across the entire arrangement of disciplines. The disciplinary organisation cuts time into chunks that suit its spatial compartmentalisations. In the disciplinary society there are working hours, leisure times, meal times, holiday seasons, bedtimes. Within each institution there is a corresponding organisation. School timetables divide activities into spaces of time that follow the room: English takes place in the classroom from 08.00-09.00 a.m., woodwork in the woodwork room from 09.00-10.00 a.m., biology in the biology room from 10.00-11.00 a.m.

The fact that discipline is not only a principle of organisation but also a principle of rationalisation means that it is a way of affirming reason. Not only are things organised in groups, they are also assembled to form a machinery. And this machinery is maximised by taking the unity to pieces and optimising the individual pieces before putting them together again. When things are organised according to a disciplinary principle, the organisation guarantees a higher reason. Not a divine but a human reason that has taken in the whole and made a plan that includes all of the parts.

Henry Ford and Frederick Taylor are usually mentioned as paradigmatic examples. From about 1913 work at the Ford factories in Detroit took place on an assembly line, i.e. the stages of production had been divided into physical spaces and spaces of time had been allotted to each part. Taylorism involves the study of time and optimising calculations, e.g. how much steel a man can lift per day. Accordingly, the Taylorian task consists in cutting away redundant time-consuming movements and breaks. From about 1930 Taylorian optimisation was linked together with the Fordian mode of production, resulting in the kind of work measurement and time optimisation that has subsequently spread to many other types of work than factory work.

Today we have *lean production* which emerged in the 1960s at the Toyota factories and is attributed to the Japanese engineer Taiichi Ohno. This is a method of analysing the sequence of operation or the sequence of service in, for instance the hospital service. Nowadays lean production looks like Taylor's optimisation inasmuch as the basic principle is to eliminate waste, *muda*, and waste is understood primarily in temporal terms. For instance, it is a waste of time that something is warehoused or awaits the finishing production. But lean differs in two significant ways. First of all, maximisation has been decentralised in the sense that it is internalised as a mentality within the individual worker. The worker is charged with the task of continuously optimising his or her area, either individually or in teams. Secondly, the optimisation of one of the sub-components may be in the way of the optimisation of the whole and in that case intervention from above is required. In this way a worker may very well be asked to work in a less efficient way, seen in isolation, if this will improve the overall flow of production within the factory. However, on the whole lean is to be seen as a way in which the disciplinary form of organisation has renewed and improved itself, rather than constituting an actual discontinuation of discipline. Lean is a way of rescuing the disciplinary mode of production at a time when competition has increased.

The organisation of projects operates on different premises which require other forms of liberties and flexibilities in order for individuals to develop solutions together and put them into practice. In projects procedures have to be developed, manuals won't do.

In practice individuals are subject to the pressure arising from the dilemma that they have to work creatively on projects with an unstable foundation and without knowing where things are going, while *at the same time* the performance of the project is evaluated as a disciplinary assignment. This is due to the fact that the disciplinary society still exists along with the project society.

In the disciplinary society school is divided into subjects – disciplines – each with their own space and time. The overall composition has been carefully considered, it is coordinated in a fashion that produces a pupil with specific skills. As opposed to what people often say about this kind of education, the purpose was not to suppress the individual but to make it stronger; to shape the desire and energy of the individual in ways that would make it a free agent. Learning the cities of one's country by heart or the table of elements, the individual was liberated as a citizen who was capable of taking action within society. The repression of play and noise and shouting was effected with the aim of empowering the individual. In the schools of the project society things are different. The project is supposed to thrive on precisely that kind of energy. The teacher's role is not to tame forces but to guide their development. The child is no longer to be taught to enjoy doing the right thing, but to be able to communicate its own will in order that a situation of negotiation between two mature people may come about.

The transition from the disciplinary society to the project society involves a transition of the way in which forces are handled: the disciplinary society would receive a force and the task was then to channel this force into the most efficient maturation. The productive force of the worker was to be channelled into the machine in order to bring about the greatest number of products. The person who maximises this process is a human engineer. Yet, since forces were moving in contrary directions, overt conflicts of interests were frequent: since the child would rather play, it had to be disciplined for the sake of its liberation. Since the worker would rather be on holiday, he had to be paid to offer his labour. The disciplinary mode of organisation manages resistance: in industry, in school, in pedagogy, in the Armed Forces, in sports clubs.

The transition to a *projectually* organised society directs these forces ahead in time. What you meet is no longer an opposition to your interests, but someone who wants to do something that you may be able to make use of. Someone to make projects with. The child wants to do something and the task is to carry that will into effect in interaction with others. Puberty, which was the greatest challenge of the pedagogy of discipline, now becomes a phase of detachment in which the child develops its own projects. The clients of the social services increasingly change from individuals with rights and duties into individuals with their own wills who want to make the best of it, and the task of the social worker is to identify wishes and desires and help the clients to turn them into realisable projects. The energy of workers' wishes and desires is not supposed to be limited to their spare time, it must be exploited in the creation, execution and running of projects. The ideal or emblematic sportsman is no longer the weight-lifter who raises the weight against the force of gravity, it is the surfer who rides the waves of the sea. The surfer does not set himself against or attempt to form the forces of nature like the sportsmen of the traditional disciplines, he exploits these forces.

The limitation of the individual by discipline was not primarily a matter of teaching the individual to limit himself or herself, which was the case with the kind of self-disciplining that was practiced in medieval monasteries. Discipline, as the predominant principle of social systems during parts of the eighteenth, nineteenth and twentieth centuries, mostly worked through external limitations. It was a matter of walls and the partition of spaces, indeed, but it was also a matter of rules. Rules would determine what was allowed to be in which places, and when, and what was to be done at what speed, etc.

In stratifying the world through rules, discipline may be said to work through a no. The teacher red-pencils the exercise book, the referee blows the whistle when fouls are committed, the maximisation of production in the factory happens through the elimination of lapses and slovenliness. Usually, when we say about a football team or a chess player that they are disciplined, we do not mean to say that they are seduced by good ideas, but that their first priority is not to make any mistakes. As we shall see later, the project society is dominated by an altogether different yes-culture in which the explicit no has completely vanished.

Rules are attached to the notion of an ideal. The rules of the housewife were attached to the ideal of the perfect family, diet rules were attached to the ideal of the healthy body, spelling rules were attached to the ideal of a faultless assignment. Ideals made an extension of judgement possible. Judgement according to a rule is a binary affair: is this acceptable or is it not? We know it from the law. Is this legal or is it illegal? But with the ideal it became possible to ask for the improvement of anything that was yet not perfect, which is to say everything real. The referee is just to make sure that the players observe the rules, he is not to judge their style of running; in gymnastics movements are assessed progressively. Such graded hierarchies submits everything to judgement: it is always possible for the body to become healthier, it is always possible for the pupil to acquire more knowledge, it is always possible for the worker to do more, it is always possible for the family to become more harmonious. Discipline normalises the world through an ideal that is not based on averages but on perfection. Normal does not mean ordinary, it means flawless. When the nurse tells me that my lungs are perfectly normal she does not mean that they work at an average in comparison with other people's lungs, but that they work impeccably.

It is important to understand that discipline and rationalisation as principles of organisation produce effects of normalisation. Obviously normalisation may be internalised as part of the way in which the world is governed and organised – e.g. by judging the performance of pupils and marking them according to how close they are to the ideal. From a social perspective it is of vital importance that regulations keep spitting out a lot of ideals as side-effects, and that these ideals – these ideas about how things ought to be – keep spreading a wide range of expectations of people to strive for perfection.

The transition to the project society does not mark a complete eradication of the system of rules and ideals. Jobs are no longer apportioned according to school performances and marks, the way it was promised by the disciplinary system. But this does not mean that proficiency at school is irrelevant.

Housing queues are no longer administered in accordance with seniority, but through acquaintances; likewise promotions in companies do not only follow seniority or performance, but also acquaintances, enthusiasm and initiative – yet this does not render performances irrelevant as a criterion of selection. The expectations of disciplinary ideals, their normativity, are still at work in everyday life, but they are sprinkled with a range of new ideals about one's capacity to combine old ideals in different ways, or a professed stance that one does not care two hoots about them. One may demonstrate a capacity to be busy while still being able to take one's time and be present to one's mind. One may behave in unhealthy ways and still have a healthy body. One may be smart without doing the homework. Or: one may give a damn about being normal and be creative and innovative instead. In addition the project society operates with an ideal of being positive and passionate and to say yes to all initiatives, e.g. a demand that is made on any dancer is that he or she feel and look as if dancing is really cool. The project society is also saturated with ideals, but it is more difficult to navigate in it because its ideals are not as systematised as in the disciplinary society. Nevertheless, it is possible to distil a systematic from the way in which the project society works, as in the analysis of the dance floor.

4.

Space in the Project Society

The transition to the project society is experienced as if something has been mixed up and all rules have vanished. Work now seems to be everywhere without any clear instructions about how a job is to be done. And it feels as if a definite 'where' has dissolved. 'Leave work at work' means: 'do not take your job with you – back home, to your weekend cottage, on holiday, in the car, back to the family' etc. In other words: leave things to the order of discipline, in which purpose, space and time all coincide. Already in 1848 Karl Marx and Friedrich Engels spoke in their Communist manifesto of how all that is solid has melted into thin air.

To explain the new in terms of a square space is typical of a disciplinary mode of thinking. The disciplinary way of organising the world happened to coincide with the Newtonian space, a quadrangular space stretched out in four dimensions. In this regard the order of discipline was a matter of tidying up the room and to designate what exactly was to happen and when. That was the kind of organisation that was imposed on the Newtonian space.

In projects connections join things that do not belong together. Consequently the project society looks very messy from the disciplinary point of view: as if a child has emptied all the drawers and tossed everything around. From the perspective of discipline the project looks undisciplined, indeed.

If we want to understand the kind of order that is after all to be found in the project society, we have to begin with something else than space: with *activity*. Holding a meeting does not depend on us actually sitting in a conference room with an agenda and a fixed decision-making procedure; it depends on what we are doing. It depends on how we speak and what we speak about, etc. That is why a dinner, a holiday and a bicycle ride may very well be meetings. It is the activity of the meeting that unfurls a meeting space, that makes a meeting a meeting, not the meeting space itself or the time or the rules of meeting.

What does it mean that activity creates space? Picture a family that arrives at the beach. As they spread out all their things on the picnic rug, they open up a space, a small base in the middle of the swarms of people. The territory is further expanded by the building of a sandcastle. And if the family starts playing ball they expand the base by opening a room for ball games.

The reason why we get so annoyed with neighbours who play loud music is that it is an invasion, as when the beach ball that drops down on the rug of a stranger on the beach, tilting his beer. The capacity of activities to open spaces may also take place in other people's spaces, opening up spaces within their spaces. By understanding spaces in terms of activity rather than in terms of walls and rules, we emphasise habitation and the act of organisation as that which constitutes a space. A girl-friend may move in technically, but she hasn't actually moved in before she brings all her stuff and starts bustling about in her particular way.

The project is an activity that opens up spaces. Of course it would be wrong to say that the project does not take place within a three-dimensional space. It does. It incorporates various three-dimensional spaces. But three-dimensional spaces are not crucial to the project, they are more like a background on which the project-activity opens a space, the way the beach is a background to games and playing. What is really at issue is a transition in principles of organisation and forms of social intercourse, which makes living in the project society an altogether different experience. The possibility of projects taking place everywhere owes to the fact that the relation between space and activity has been changed. The difference may be illustrated in the following way: At the theatre the play takes place on the stage. The theatre constitutes the framework that has stretched out a space in which the play may unfold. The activity of the play takes place as the actors go about reciting lines they have learned in advance and staging movements that have been pre-arranged into fixed sequences. In comparison the project society is more like an improvised street theatre: the nature of its performance, its activity makes it possible to open a theatre at any street corner. It cannot rely on firing off well-rehearsed lines in pre-arranged sequences, it has to remain open to and act in accordance with all the chance events that may occur in the street.

Just as projects have always been around, the kind of relation between space and activity in which space is created by an activity, rather than space being a stage for an activity to take place, has always existed. What distinguishes the project society is that this kind of relation is starting to become the most dominating relation between space and activity, i.e. that today we are living in ways in which we unfurl spaces through our projects. That is the reason why we often get the sense that work, leisure, school, health and the individual is all over the place.

One of the consequences of space being created by activities is that the question of inclusion and exclusion comes across in new ways. The question of who is part of the project and who isn't is not determined on the basis of who is inside and who is outside. In fact it cannot be defined unambiguously in binary terms. There are no rules in the project of who is in and who is out – if one wants to join one has to come forward, one has to offer activities that are similar to what the others are doing – as in dancing.

The so-called project management that takes place in the public sector as well as in private companies is not an actual project the way it is described in this book, but it forms a part of the transition from plan to project in which assignments are redefined as a kind of projects in which one cannot depend on a repetition of the same, but still tries to institute a disciplinary framework management with lines of procedure and pre-defined aims.

In pure projects membership is not graduated. One joins as a team or an individual player by throwing oneself into the game, as sports commentators put it, i.e. by doing something, communicating, by creating chances, hitting on ideas, suggesting things and realising things. It is possible to draw maps of the project society, but they must be based on activities and not on rules. But the fact that these maps are superimposed on other structures of authority just makes the picture even more complicated. It may be a given that the producer appointed by the theatre manager is part of the project, but his role varies according to what he is doing. And certainly – because there are things that are certain in the project society – unpaid producer assistants will join the project and resign from it all according to what they are doing.

The former is quite important: projects may be described in their pure form but they always take place on top of the stratifications and laws that were brought about by the disciplinary society. Projects may be engaged with the intention of reaching aims that one tried to reach by disciplinary means, but this takes place on the basis of another form of organisation. Of course the aim in football, which is not a traditionally disciplined game, is still to win the match. Likewise companies organised by projects have not abandoned the idea of profit – on the contrary. The project is an alternative way of cashing in traditional objectives. Discipline would seek to organise its way out of problems through a detailed plan and a number of instructions. Instead the project society strives to mobilise individuals to get them to create something themselves. There are still instructors (coaches) and managers, but their role as project managers is a different one: it is to organise things on the basis of the logic I am trying to describe here, including the task of inducing individuals to engage in self-realising activities within existing projects.

The project de-differentiates the spaces established by the disciplinary society – including its institutions – and re-differentiates them in different projects. From the perspective of the law and discipline the project cuts across the established order. From the perspective of the project it is a matter of forming planes across spaces rather than merely jumbling things together, it is a matter of transgressions that are not actual violations. Once again it goes that projects do not unfold within a historyless space, but within a society that is regulated by law and ordered by discipline. Inevitably, this is something that affects the projects. As said, without disciplines a project would not be cross-disciplinary, i.e. it would not be stepping across disciplines.

Needless to say, the transition in relations between activity and space is a transition that architecture has to deal with too. Architecture has played a decisive role in connection with discipline: discipline intended to order space to make it controllable. The problem of a ruler may be that a closed space, e.g. a city, may have an order of its own that is out of contact with its formal administration. That is why Napoleon ordered his troops to destroy the inner gates of Cairo, to make it accessible to the central power of France. In the 1860s Baron Hausmann rebuilt Paris by laying out grand boulevards across the city in order to make it possible to survey the masses. Disciplinary control came about by increasing the visibility of the central power, from the commander to teacher.

In general discipline is about consolidating power within forms. The activity that opens up a space may for instance open up a piece of land as a territory. A territory may be fragile but a strong form may be erected around it. The Germans who put up a windshield on the beach may do so not only to shelter from the wind, but also to keep their territory together without having to sustain it through an activity. When the family goes swimming, the borders of the territory are still there for everyone to see. In addition disciplinary control strives to implement itself through inward architectural activities, i.e. to create lines of command and to establish spaces dedicated to certain functions, and to maintain this internal architecture through forms.

The projectual form of organisation gradually gains ground on a basis that is already shaped by disciplinary control. The architectural shaping of a space effects a slowing down of the advance of the project – or at least it constitutes a condition the project has to reckon with. One place in which the project became omnipresent in the 1970s and 1980s was in schools. It was not enough for pupils to learn certain skills by heart anymore, now they also had to learn how to work together on isolated projects. Clearly this was so because schools were part of a society that was going through a transition to the project society while at the same time they comprised the institutional body in which individuals had to (and still have to) learn how to get on in the project society.

In the 1970s and '80s the problem was (and remains so today) that schools were not architecturally designed for the new kind of pedagogy, they were built for class instruction of the examinatory kind. To the extent that new schools were built these were furnished with seminar rooms, as was the case, for instance, in Denmark with about forty planned schools and the university centres of Roskilde and Aalborg. Subsequently a disciplinary wave struck back at the pedagogy that challenged discipline, but a number of preparatory and secondary schools with passageways and rooms designed for projects are still standing – and they are still used for group projects.

The transition to the pedagogy of the project society involved more than working on projects in groups. It also included a more dialogic form of teaching; pupils were allowed to say something themselves and little by little it was also possible for them to communicate with other people than the teacher, i.e. directly with other pupils. For this purpose the arrangement of tables in straight lines was no longer appropriate because pupils were facing the backs of their classmates. Initially an architectural solution was sought for by rearranging the furniture in the shape of a horseshoe. Project corners were also created, e.g. a corner in the class room for reading, a corner for group work or a corner for computers.

The architecture of the school in the project society is different. The best example in Denmark is a school north of

Copenhagen, Hellerup Skole. The school has been built with a library at the centre and a great flight of stairs where people may sit down. The school is dominated by open spaces with many corners and recesses where pupils may work on their projects. There are class rooms for the instruction of basic skills like reading, writing and arithmetic, but the walls are movable. The school reflects what the architecture of the project is supposed to deliver: large passageways in which people can meet each other while on the move. On the other hand a large passageway is not enough as there is too much noise to carry out the projects. The individual must be able to enter into the passageway, stay there and, if necessary, withdraw a little. Still, it is crucial that other activities can make contact with the projects. The corridor with conference rooms behind closed doors is the architecture of bureaucracy where it is always decided in advance who is supposed to be at the meeting. But the project moves between openness and withdrawal, between the creation of networks and the activity of projects, and that is what the architects of the project society have to include in their considerations. Finally any room has to be reshapable; users must always be able to reshape space according to different functions, e.g. the walls may be movable or all furniture mounted on wheels. In general a transition like that may be described as a transition from form to formation.

Schooling in the disciplinary society was like a mould, a moulding of the individual. In the school of the project society the individual is to be assisted in the process of expressing herself and in that way give shape to herself. In keeping with the rest of the project society it is crucial pupils learn to give shape to themselves as one of the basic qualifications that are required in the project society is the ability to constantly re-shape oneself; the kind of person who comes in a fixed shape produced by an educational institution remains passive in terms of self-creation, and that is risky business.

In terms of architecture this means that forms must be re-formable by activities. The ideal is to give form to things in ways that are conducive to perpetual remodelling. However, in this age of transition architects are rarely given the opportunity of designing a building for projects from scratch. For one, there are still many bureaucratic, industrial or hierarchical aspects to be taken into account. Secondly, the project society often has to adapt itself to and rebuild the architecture of the disciplin-ary society. In this respect the architects of the project society seem to have a marked preference for a particular part of the disciplinary society, industry. The reason is that old indus-trial buildings and storehouses have large spaces which may be turned into office landscapes. Within these landscapes confe-rence rooms may be constructed with glass walls with drawable curtains, demonstrating a large degree of transparency while providing the participants of meetings with the possibility of auditive and visual shielding. The crucial point is that indivi-duals are enabled to meet across departments and start projects together, accidentally or on purpose. This also requires the work space to be architecturally arranged in a manner that centres on passageways, as opposed to reducing passage to a matter of time consuming transport between stations.

To understand the project society and projectual people it is important to bear in mind that they are not merely sociological categories or terms in the discipline of work sociology. This means that a concurrence of the same type of challenges and provocations can be traced within different disciplinary organisations. In this way the repeatability of discipline is challenged on its ability to eliminate accidental occurrences of projectual ways of exploiting contingency. The ability of a discipline to repeat itself is challenged by the demand for a high degree of sensitivity in regard to that which is to be organised as well as by the demand for flexibility and rapid readjustment. It all started with a shaking of the bars of disciplines within the first half of the twentieth century, which erupted as a revolt in the 1960s and 1970s, as in the case of dancing. But all the flipping and the tripping of the revolt did not end up as flipping and tripping. The revolt against discipline came down to us in a way that cooperates with discipline, expands but also transgresses it – which we may refer to as the project.

The showdown with disciplinary pedagogy, for instance, followed this pattern: first, a democratic pedagogy demanding that everybody be equal emerged in the 1970s as a counter to disciplinary upbringing. Not only did men and women have to be equal, children were also to be on equal terms with adults, which is why they would no longer address their parents as 'mum' and 'dad' but use their personal names instead. This egalitarian revolt against hierarchical control is not the project society. The project society involves a pedagogy of competence in which parents and children are not equals, yet raising the child is about guiding energy into expression rather than taming it. The road from the democratic and egalitarian pedagogy to the pedagogy of competence goes through a number of disciplinary retro-movements that react against all that the revolt is incapable of. People react against the notion that children are supposed to be like adults from the very beginning of their lives and roll back to a pedagogy whose aim it is to shape the individual. Gradually the project society comes about in such exchanges between pedagogical philosophies: now it is a matter of shaping the children to be able to shape themselves by teaching them to be assertive, to take initiatives and to negotiate. Children are still unformed, yet it won't do just to impose a form upon them. They have to be supported in their development of the art of self-creation.

The birth of homo projectus owes to a reconfiguration of the ways of being human. The fact that the project is not simply a social trend, although it sometimes seems trendy to be connected to projects, becomes clear if we turn to consider a number of organisational systems that are very different from the ones we have looked at so far. Turning to the development of football, for instance, it appears that similar reconfigurations of time and space take place as a challenge to disciplinary football. A football player is not simply thrown into project contracts in work sociological terms – it is far more important that he adapts his way of playing to the same challenges of discipline that we find in other areas: the ability to exploit unforeseen events, adjustability, flexibility and the ability to change along with his object. The modern football player is a projectual human especially on the field. Let's take a closer look at the development of football for a moment.

In the thirteenth century football took place as a match between two towns, and the game was about getting a ball through the other town's gates by more or less violent means. There was no delimited field and there was no clear distinction between spectators and participants in the match, or what made a person an actual participant; nor was there any clear definition of what was allowed and what was not allowed. The fact that it was difficult to tell audience and participants apart bears a resemblance to today's dance floors: it all depended on the individual's activity. At this time in the history of football the game had not gone through a disciplinary structuralisation like today's football and dancing, however, and hence the movements within the game did not transgress any pre-established form.

With industrialisation and urbanisation football (i.e. ball games that are played not by horse but by foot) moved within city boundaries where an artificial space was created especially for this activity. The soccer field was born. Different rules applied to the game at the public schools in England within the first half of the nineteenth century. Tactics were simple, commonly revolving around strategies like filling the space close to the goal with people to block the ball and the rival team from breaking through.

In 1840 a set of rules was written down at the public school of Rugby that allowed the goalkeeper to use his hands and to queer the patch of the opponent. Those rules were to become the foundation of the game of rugby as we know it today, and they differed from the way football was played at Eton. In 1863 nine English football clubs joined up and founded the Football Association on Eton's rules.

However, this did not bring about any actual disciplining of the game of football. All of the ten fieldsmen were chasing the ball as we know it from children's soccer today. The first measures of discipline came about by assigning players to different positions and functions on the field with the purpose of maximising the performance of the team. The players were to stick to a team plan.

The disciplining of the football team was equal to the disciplining of the army and factory workers. It involved 1) a spatial differentiation of the field into specific spheres of activity, 2) a functional differentiation, i.e. a division of labour, 3) the establishment of a chain conveyor. A disciplinary system of organisation was installed on the basis of these differentiations. Playing in a disciplinary fashion meant that you would keep to your designated space and your assignments and duties in relation to the transport of the ball.

The earliest control systems corresponded to what we would refer to today as a three-figure combination of 2-3-5 ('the pyramid'), i.e. two defenders, three midfielders and five strikers. Bit by bit, however, this proved to be a rather weak structure when playing more defensive teams. The inner wings were drawn back and in the period from 1925 to 1950 teams subscribed to the so-called WM-system, i.e. 3-2-2-3. Among other things, this was the system with which Italy won the world cup in 1934.

The crucial point to our present concern is that organisation was thought primarily along the lines of man-to-man relations: any player's assignment was a specific opponent within a specific space of the field. The M-formation of the defence corresponded to the W-formation of the rival team's offence. The advantage of spatial and functional differentiation was that it was energy-saving: transport was handed over to the network, or as the term goes in football, it was a matter of letting the ball do the work.

The strength of the WM-system was its stability. This was also where it was challenged by opponent teams. In the 1950s when the Hungarian national coach Marton Bukovi needed a strong centre forward he moved this position back to the midfield and used him as a playmaker there instead. Now the midfield comprised five players in a 3-5-2-formation. The two offensive midfielders were then supposed to assist the strikers whenever the team took possession of the ball, transforming the formation into a 3-3-4. By separating players from zones, i.e. by allowing players to operate in several zones, the old systems were challenged on their mobility. Now the choice was between man-to-man marking and zonal marking as these were no longer the same thing.

In the course of the 1960s and 1970s different systems were employed to stem the mobility of the 3-5-2-system and the even more dynamic Brazilian system of 4-2-4. One of these was the Italian *catenaccio*-tactics, the door bolt imported from the Swiss national coach Karl Rappan's chain system (*le verrou*): through a rearrangement of the players one player was freed: the sweeper, who was to sweep the area in front of the goal. This was a disciplinarian tactics that aimed always to secure a 1-0 victory. Yet the challenges of the programmatic systems did not end with this.

At the time when hands were let go in dancing, there were experiments in football with an even more flexible system: Dutch Total Football. The ideal is that each player is capable of thinking as the entire team as well as playing all positions. As soon as a player moves on the field another player takes over his position. In this way the team creates a greater degree of mobility without having to run that much faster. For instance, when a defender joins an attack, the entire team adjusts in principle by changing positions in order that the defender does not have to return to the defence and gets to play the striker position for a while. The dilemma between man and zone was solved by resorting to a third principle of organisation: movement.

In practice players are not smart enough to play Total Football, even though attempts have been made between the chains, e.g. by Rinus Michels in Ajax Amsterdam between 1965 and 1971, and in Barcelona by the same coach between 1971 and 1975, and by the Dutch national team in 1974 and from 1984 to 1992. At the same time the disciplinary system kept developing ways of stemming this mobility, and teams ended up with systems that were mobile at a more local level, e.g. Barcelona's forward line in the years between 1988-96, Laudrup-Romario-Stoichkof.

Today the challenges of the disciplinarian systems in football have come down as a mixture between a kind of spatial-functionally differentiated field-position football and the movements of Total Football, which may be referred to as motion football. Generally this involves variations of the 4-4-2-formation with a great obligation of individual enterprise, e.g. 'the diamond', which may also be described as a 4-1-2-1-2. In comparison with the 'industrialised' field-position game, teams in this way compete more on the basis of mobility than on stamina. It is not just a matter of "letting the ball do the work", i.e. exploiting the chains of transport in order to save energy. It is about increasing the speed of movement which requires both the ball and the players to move around faster than before. Three-figure combination systems seem increasingly outdated as a tool to describe the actual game because the notion of defence-midfield-offence belongs to the old way of picturing transportation. One way of expressing this is to say that the players are fitted up with an anchor rather than a space. The length of the leash of this anchor depends on physical fitness, speed and the position of the anchor. In a sense all players have turned into liberos, anchored within a space yet mobile. This only works if the individual player does more than he is supposed to – or rather: it requires that the assignment of the players is redefined as an expectation of creative performances. It is no longer possible to play the full back position without having to run the length of the entire field, one is also expected to take the initiative, to take part in building up the attack, to be a *createur*.

Field-position football lost the command when it lost the control of space. The challenge of the stable by means of flexibility was a matter of removing the control of space by means of activity. The offside position illustrates the battle between discipline and project: the defence tries to control space while the offence tries to open up space by means of orthogonal attempts of subversion. In the project society all players must be able to open up spaces.

The Argentine football coach Helenio Herrera was the one to take the credit for the play-safe style of *catenaccio* when he introduced it in Inter Milano in 1960. He had left his job as the coach of Barcelona. Yet, before leaving he had taught the Catalans something that was ahead of his time: the one-touch game. He had changed the game from a game of possession to a game of movement. These are different ways of comprehending safety than we are used to, i.e. as something that comes about through the control of space. Instead safety is comprehended in terms of remaining in a state of transition. As we shall see in chapter six this is a new approach to security, something that relates to the passage, something that distinguishes the project society.

The challenge of the stable, controllable and programmatic mode of organisation that we know by the name of discipline, whose strengths are repetition and the elimination of chance occurrences, takes place within a wide range of areas simultaneously. The disciplinary mode of organisation is challenged on four different matters: it is challenged on its *sensitivity towards its object and its capacity to adapt to it*, whether it be a customer or an opponent, on its capacity to *adjust itself to new conditions*, on *flexibility* and on its capacity to *incorporate and exploit contingency*. This occurs more or less simultaneously within the realms of sport, dancing, the social services, warfare, pedagogics, architecture, professional organisation, the combating of disease, coupling... in short within all the bodies that used to be institutions but are now understood according to the logic of the project and the concepts that come with it: temporariness, passage, connection, network, activity. It is not only institutions that are going through a transformation, it also applies to the very grating that keeps institutions apart.

5.

Time in the Project Society

The Medieval Father Augustine said that he knew very well what time was if only he wasn't asked about it; then he started thinking about it. To comprehend time may be quite hard, but this should not keep us from saying something about time, especially about how the project relates to time. Different activities entail different ways of approaching or living out time. This results in the presence of different kinds of time: a physical time, a mathematical time and an experienced time. The sun rises and sets and in that way it frames the time of the day. This is physical time. However, if we start accumulating days into weeks or dividing the day into hours and noting the hour and minute of sunrise and sunset, we are dealing with a mathematical time. We have thrown a mathematical grid upon time.

Time was mathematised in the European Renaissance. Daytime still comprised the time from cockcrow to dusk, but a day as such was determined as a fixed number of hours of equal length. In summer there are more hours of daylight than during the winter, but in spite of physical changes the duration of an hour remains fixed. Part of the scientification of everyday life and the modernisation of society and modes of thinking consists in the increasing predominance of a mathematical comprehension of time. As it happened to space, a system of co-ordinates was forced on time, giving us the calendar, the time table, etc.

In addition to physical and mathematical time, it is possible to make an outline of time as experienced time. A single hour may be experienced very differently according to what one is doing. If you are bored, time passes slowly. This is because we have become used to a comprehension of time in terms of space, as something that runs through an extension of space. But experienced time does not really run through any spatial extension, rather time is extended by what we are doing. In-between finishing what we were doing and anticipating what we are about to do, a stretch of time is extended by what we are doing at the moment. The child who is busy playing, absorbed in the task of assembling tracks for a toy train, is outside mathematical time. The adult who is busy cooking needs a timer to remind him when to take the bread out of the oven because he is busy chopping the vegetables in order to make the salad, in order to complete the entire meal. In situations when we are busy doing something we experience time in a non-mathematical way. By contrast, when we are waiting for the clock to strike five, the time when Daddy returns, mathematical time comes to the fore. Philosophers would refer to this description of experienced time as phenomenology and occasionally they refer to experienced time as 'duration'.

The disciplinary mode of controlling and organising the world and the way we interact with each other is organised in accordance with mathematical time. It imposes a co-ordination system of time on the co-ordination system of space, in that way shaping a way of living in which activities take place within specific spaces of time – working hours, breaks, dinner, time for brushing the teeth, bedtime, etc. It is this particular way of co-ordinating space and time that makes it possible for us to start calculating processes in order to optimise them. It is also this kind of co-ordination that facilitates large scale planning of production plants, armies or entire populations that are co-ordinated through censuses, elections or total vaccinations. Or on a smaller scale, enabling different classes to use the school gymnasium at different times.

Of course people who live in a disciplinary society also experience time. How do they experience time? On the basis of *repetition*. The experience of the return of things, of doing things over and over again, forms life according to a specific rhythm. Institutions have each their own rhythm with several variations of repetition. One does not eat the same every day, but it is always the same person cooking the food at the same time of the day. All institutions are constructed by routines, which, in turn, are planned according to what is most economical, healthy, profitable or successful. In the jargon of sports, people speak of a team as ingrained with 'automatisms', i.e. patterns learned by heart that enable players to do something faster than if they had to invent it from scratch, and which is, above all, more safe.

Security and *repetition* are intimately connected in the experience of time: tomorrow will be more or less the same. Providing for one's own safety is therefore also a matter of making sure that things remain the same – that we still have the house, the job, the same friends and the bridge club. The condition of protecting oneself by securing the repetition of things is that repetition is securable in the first place. It is; within a disciplinary, industrial society. That is why the disciplinary society is ruled by the Stoic virtue of *constantia*: always staying the same makes it possible for people to rely on each other. This is not a matter of course in the project society. Why not?

The most important reason is that repetition is no longer possible. When activities unfold as projects, they unfold as something that does not repeat itself.

The virtue of staying the same also disintegrates pari passu with the impossibility of repetition. There is a connection between the prevalent ways of structuring and organising space, time, actions and relations and the normative expectations to the individuals within them. People are still rewarded for behaving in ways that suit the prevalent form of organisation; the only difference is that the change to a projectual form of organisation has produced new expectations to individuals.

Society's detachment from the era of discipline comes with a form of organisation that makes it impossible to tame accidental occurrences and cause the individual to enter into a planned process in predictable ways. Instead everybody is competing about exploiting the accidental to their own advantage. Back in time when it was possible to found one's factory on the same Ford T Model year after year, the organisational task was a matter of getting different people to do the same thing simultaneously. But as fashion changes and customers now want a new colour every second year and a new model once in a while, one has to adjust to the randomness of such whims. If at the same time there are a large number of companies competing on adjustment, competition shifts to be a matter of who is the best in grasping what the customers want. Eventually it is no longer enough to produce a fine car, one also has to interpret the signs of the times and the consumers, and above all one must be able to readjust very quickly. In a process like that it is no longer enough to base one's production on repetition, one has to base it on change. How do you organise a mode of production based on change rather than repetition? The answer is: through projects.

The project is an appreciated form of organisation when the pressure of change rises exactly because its activity is not based on how you used to do things, but on the ability of individuals to invent things on the basis of present conditions. The project never repeats itself, it is a new project every time. Nor will any given project ever become the foundation of a repetition; it will always be the springboard of a new project.

Our relation to time changes the moment the world is no longer kept going by repetitions and rhythms. Now it is the activity of the project that extends the duration of the project instead. The project exists only as long as there is activity, it does not carry on just because time goes by. When involved in a project, time is unfurled by activity – just as space is unfurled by activity. That is why it is possible for projects not only to take place everywhere but also to take place at all times. Whenever you are speaking of what is relevant to the project, whenever you are doing something in relation to the project, you are actually busy working on it. The time of the projected is unfurled as experienced time; it is not sustained by any framework of when and where. Projects may have deadlines, but that is the influence of a disciplinarian framework; it is not part of the logic of the project. Playing in the schoolyard is not done just because the bell rings and the break ends, and one has not completed a thesis just because time is up. You only bring an end to it.

Since the project is not based on repetition it is unplanable. This does not mean that it is impossible to squeeze it into disciplinary categories, like phases or by subdividing it into prejects and projects. But in its pure form the project is as impossible to premeditate as a conversation, what is to be said and done, and it does not submit to mathematical control.

Just as importantly, since the project has no foundation in repetition, it does not only raise the question of 'how', but also of 'what', 'who' and 'whereto'. Planning was a matter of laying down activities, step by step, before they were carried out. With the project it is the other way round: Whatever is to be done, how to do it and the criteria of evaluation are defined by the activities. The fact that projects establish their own criteria for success also means that projects tend to legitimise themselves.

The activity of projects estimates its success in a backward manner. It is only afterwards that it becomes possible to make a reconstruction of which activities were actually useful and what was a waste, when one was actually working on the project and when one wasn't. Discussing a particular composition at a dinner actually turned out to be of great importance, whereas the week we spent working with those Norwegians turned out to be a waste of time. In its ideal form it is impossible to check out the project according to any standard because it creates its own standards. A theatre project may certainly produce a bad play but this does not mean that it can be pointed out where exactly someone made a mistake.

The release of the project society from traditional, repetitive, synchronised time into projects that open up lapses of time within project-born, temporary communities also constitutes a disruption of sequential time. Sequential time involved a consistency guaranteed by a succession. Something would cohere in time through a before and an after. The history of a nation is put together by individuals succeeding each other.

What causes things that succeed each other to cohere? The *narrative* is a grasp that ties points together to form a thread. Just as a movie or a picture book is not merely a matter of images succeeding each other, life is not experienced as disparate events, but as something that coheres. Narratives involve accentuations in time of cause and effect that make life look like a chain of events. A curriculum vitae is by far the dullest version of a life because it merely lists results in a chronological chain, without indicating any upheavals, reasons or painful efforts.

Traditionally such narratives were collective. To the extent that one had any projects, it was with the aim of entering one's own time. One wanted to be the grocer in order to be the grocer of the town and find one's place there. Above the town's narratives were national narratives, tying larger groups together. Below the town's narratives were individual narratives, tying the events of a life together and interweaving it with the major narratives. Collectivity and repetition are significant in these narratives: identities are tied together by the repetitive experiences of individuals and their narratives of these experiences. That guy over there is so and so. We are like this and that. Not to mention those guys.

Individuals and collectives are partially disentangled from identity by the absence of repetition in the projectual mode of organisation. The fact that you are constantly working with new people in new projects makes it easier to keep adopting new roles. The fact that companies keep replacing their employees because they are employed in temporary projects causes them to lose their identity. This increases the need to tell the story of the company's identity together – and if narratives are no longer pre-given, they have to be created and brought into play. On the one hand, the absence of collective narratives dilutes the values of the company, the organisation, the town, but on the other hand, the company, the organisation, the town are also free to invent new values, or at best incorporate new values.

In a way the same goes for the individual. While people

speak a lot about self-government in companies, they fail to notice how the self is torn away from itself in projects without any community to confirm the self. Freud claims that the self is created through conflicts. Now and then all this talk of self-government also overlooks how the effacement of frameworks eliminates the borders and boundaries which used to be used by the self to create itself out of conflict.

Once again this is a hazard and an opportunity at one and the same time. On the one hand, the basic psychological safety of remaining the same is missing. On the other hand, the fact that people are no longer forced into the same narratives of themselves and each other opens a greater scope of opportunity. Without a doubt the ability of keeping the self together through the narrative of the self becomes a crucial psychological skill, lest one should disintegrate into nothingness. There are freedoms and dangers in any project that turns into a space without the attachment of any unifying time thread. Paradoxically, the projectual human may experience the absence of structure as a repetitive, monotonous humdrum. This is because the absence of a unifying thread may also be experienced as an absence of progress. Singles who keep throwing themselves into new love projects after every wrecked attempt at starting a relationship may begin to experience this as repetition intruding upon their lives as a condition rather than the individual having made a conscious choice of living life without a steady relationship. The same may happen to freelancers who keep throwing themselves into new projects and still think that it is the same all over again. Both examples involve conscious choices in the sense of something that one engages in and devotes oneself to. The project society is not something the individual may choose or choose to do without; it is an increasingly urgent condition. Yet the way in which one deals with this kind of relation to time, space and repetition may be a conscious choice.

When God called in sick, people started talking of a problem of contingency. Man had to get used to the fact that nothing was necessary anymore, that everything was contingent, happening by chance. As Nietzsche pointed out, the crisis of values and nihilism in the nineteenth century was closely connected with the idea that there is no God.

The problem of contingency that the individuals of the project society are faced with does not (only) involve the absence of necessity, but (also) the absence of constancy. The fact that everything is transitory is a new trial of strength: Who is able to endure jumping from one ice floe to another?

It also creates new conditions: Above all one has to adjust to the curiosity that 'ad hoc' has become a fundamental condition and to the agreed collective arrangement that everyone expects all things and relations to be made on a short term basis which will quickly expire. There is no reason to invest a lot effort or emotion or energy in a thing or an acquaintance if the condition of rapid restructurings causes one to keep moving and replacing stuff. On the other hand, there may be all the more reason to apply aesthetic or experience-related criteria:

She is a good friend right now. These are my needs right now. My current boyfriend is... The fact that you cannot be sure of anything is the only thing you can be sure of.

As the sociologist Max Weber has pointed out, the development of capitalism was brought on the high road of success by Protestantism: The notion that it was impossible for you to know if you were predestined for salvation or damnation, but that it was still possible to call forth prospective signs that might be deciphered and interpreted in life on earth, brought about an enterprising and hard-working kind of people – as long as success in the world of business could be interpreted as a sign of being one of God's elect. In the project society it is the absence of constancy that may give an impetus to the forces of productivity: The fact that we have no idea if we need you for the next project, let alone the fact that we don't know the criteria we intend to use for our selection of employees, provokes you not only to do a proper job, but to think of something that is even better than that. With this we have come to the question of how people act within the project society.

6.

Acting in the Project Society

The project is delimited in two ways: It is temporary and it is not the only project. A project does not fill up all of one's working time, love life or hobby room; it merely opens work, love or play in various ways. That is why one may have many projects that may be opened at different occasions. If you know that a project is about to expire, it may be a sensible thing to have other irons in the fire to make sure that there will always be other projects to do whenever one project ends.

It is common property that the so-called unemployed, as they are referred to within the logic of discipline in which working and not-working is a binary matter of inclusion, apply for several jobs at the time. It may also be common knowledge that singles are operating according to a similar multipolar project activity. The difference is that the latter is not to be advertised. In certain respects the logic of the project society works in a way in which the intended function is destroyed as soon as it is pointed out. You have to act as if the contact you make with another person is unique. In other words you have to pretend that your motives are of a disciplinary nature while being thrown upon a projectual logic.

The same goes for the work place. Although permanent employment still exists the logic of the project may have slipped in anyway: Anyone who keeps the same job for more than three years will stick to the pot like burnt milk. Hence you have to make sure to move on to another job before it is too late. Everybody knows that, including the employer. Yet at the same time you cannot ask for an afternoon off on the grounds that you have to go somewhere else for a job interview. If someone finds an application in the company's printer, it is a sign of co-worker having offended against the team spirit, although he may be true to the spirit of the times.

Why seek out new projects while still being busy with some? Because current projects expire or turn into blind alleys. Because the mantra of movement has replaced the praise of routine. And because the increasing difficulty or impossibility of repetitions has foiled the transmutation of routine into a normative state of affairs: My, are you still working there? You're not stuck, are you? But it is just as important to note that a positive feedback mechanism is activated within the mode of the transitory and the uncertain: When you have no idea of what is going to come of it, you better search for something more, or say yes to whatever is offered. This generates a logic of overbooking, which gives a new meaning to the word 'yes'. As people no longer say no in the project society, the significance of a 'yes' is hollowed out. 'That sounds interesting', 'let's do that one day', 'yes, I'd like to join you on that' ... all of this means no more than a temporary yes, which may be annulled at any time. When individuals start seeing through the hollowness of the 'yes', that's when the positive feedback sets in: Deals are made with more people than are needed for the project, you say yes to more than you have time for and later you cancel redundant jobs. Knowing that everyone does the same, the tendency is reinforced and people say yes to even more with even less worth of promise.

The one who enters a dating site on the Internet for the first time may think she has come to an amorous Mecca. All these people proposing themselves. All these people saying yes. However, this luring impression lasts only as long as one hasn't worked out that it is the logic of the project that is at it again. Everyone overbooks. When communicating with people, one must assume that they communicate with several others in the same way, even if the object of the communication – to find the one and only – excludes the possibility of others. But since you don't know what it may lead to, and you know that everyone else does the same, only assigning an additional booking to any endearing word, you will assume the role of a retard if you refuse to do the same. But woe betide him who accidentally makes it explicit.

The same logic may be observed in a wide range of other areas. On the house swapping market, where one may exchange holiday homes with people from other countries, people usually send out inquiries to a lot of people at the same time. Accordingly, if you respond positively to an inquiry, you cannot be sure that a deal will actually be made. A proposal is not a genuine offer, but a probable offer. Not only does the project society undo safety and planning, it also reverts promises to probabilities.

When considering another condition that any projectual person has to deal with, probability steps to the fore even more: that is, the condition projects are temporary. Temporariness is not a condition that has suddenly occurred. It forms the activity of the project as a climate of uncertainty and indeterminacy. As it is, temporariness lays it down as a condition of life that one has to keep passing on. You have to find other ice floes to jump onto before this one melts. This places the *passage* at the very centre of the activities of projectual people, as a mode that shapes the choice of and the activities within projects. For instance, in the world of research it is quite common that once a researcher has received funding for one research project, he or she has to spend a great deal of time working out new research projects and apply for their funding while actually being hired to do the first one. Bureaucracy was commonly accused of being inefficient because it had to be just and to operate according to fixed procedures. The modes of distribution in the project society are hardly more efficient, but the inefficiency consists in something else: in the activity of the project being structured by the consciousness of passage.

The condition of temporariness does not only cause rupture wherever there used to be a sequential time structure. The problem of passage is not just a question of *how* one gets to the next project, it is a state of general confusion about *where* one may pass to altogether. The condition of temporariness advances like a climate of uncertainty that causes everyone to start betting on all horses. In turn, the fact that everyone is betting on all horses generates the kind of relations in which everyone says yes without being sure how much they actually mean it. There will be time enough to find out about that. For the same reason anybody's yes means no more than may be taken back again on the spur of the moment, out of common courtesy or out of indecision or because that was actually what they had in mind in the first place. The widespread culture of cancellations is not only due to the use of mobile phones, it owes to the fact that the temporary yes has become a normal mode of contact, it owes to the fact that the passage has installed itself as a chronic condition.

The passages have always been dangerous. The three Billy Goats Gruff had to cross a bridge, the Israelites had to return home from Egypt. Something could go wrong in the passage. That is why the passage has traditionally been classed with things that were removed from everyday experience for fear that it might disturb the order of society. The passage is arranged by society, but in the form of an outside within society. The exam does not take place in everyday class teaching. The testing of the examinee takes place in another room in which people speak with one another in a different way. She enters as a pupil and exits as a student.

Passages may be necessary to maintain the order of society, and after the passage things fall back into place through repetition. The manhood test was to take place in the forest; he went out as a boy and returned as a man. The first time a female had intercourse was just as important. It was important that it took place with the right man – but it could go wrong, it might turn out that it was not her 'first time', or that it was impossible to go through with the sex act. That is why the first intercourse was to take place on a journey, a honeymoon trip: At best she went out as a girl and came home as a woman.

A passage represents a transition between positions within society. They occur on rare occasions and when one emerges from the passage one has definitely arrived in the new position. One has changed jobs and is now working in a new place. Anthropologists refer to this theme as liminality, borderline situations. In the project society the passage has become ubiquitous. Not only because passages between projects occur with great frequency, but also because the passage has doubled as a state of consciousness within and between the projects.

The permanence of the passage problem means that you have to choose your projects with great care. Firstly, the activity of your projects must lead to something that is visible to others and easy to understand. Paradoxically, projects are expected to lead to something new and be recognisable at the same time. Secondly, you have to make sure to put your signature on the project for everyone to see that you are or were part of it. And thirdly, you have to pick your projects in proportion to the likelihood of accomplishing something spectacular.

Thus, the passage is not only a problem, it is also an element of distinction: The one who demonstrates an ability to move between projects with great ease rises above the crowd. Everybody wants to join forces with a person like that or to become part of his or her projects. On top of that, the very aspect of having projects works like a billboard that facilitates one's passage to other projects: The one that was used last time may be used again. That is why it is better to be abused than not used at all – which introduces exploitation as something positive that individuals are ready to compete for. Moreover it is an element of distinction to be able to connect things that do not belong together (i.e. all the things that were kept apart by the disciplinary society). You may assert yourself by transgressing established borders. Projects are better if they are transversal, transnational, cross-cultural, cross-territorial – cross-disciplinary – than if they stick to disciplines.

The more one joins that kind of projects the easier it gets to keep passing on. Your network expands and you sparkle like the coming man who refuses any form of limitation. One may wonder if it doesn't take certain skills, e.g. proficiency in a discipline, to take part in transgressive projects. This doesn't seem to be the case. In educational institutions whose pedagogy is shaped by the transition from disciplinary to projectual forms of organisation, pupils are taught to be cross-disciplinary from the very beginning, to create projects and to communicate. It is true that society needs more than exclusively transversal connection workers. It needs people who put things on the shelves, who sort things and institute basic structures which the projectual workers may then transgress. But this does not prevent individuals from pursuing their happiness as cross-disciplinary beings from the very beginning, nor does it prevent educational institutions from meeting this demand.

If you acquire a talent for passing on to new projects by unfurling all of your activities in projects, does this then mean that you may feel safe and secure? Not if by security one means that you can count on the perpetual repetition of the same: That the farm will still be there tomorrow, that the cows must be milked again, that the factory continues to exist, that there will be work to be done, that next year is your silver wedding, that you are going to take the children to the same school once again tomorrow morning. The distinguishing feature of the project society is that it is not based on repetition but on change, which is why it cannot offer any security in the usual sense of the word. It offers something instead: We cannot rest assured that the existing state of things will last, but we can rest assured that it will not last. Accordingly, we may adjust to the existing state of things in such a way that the likelihood of something new occurring is greater than the likelihood of things remaining the same. I cannot promise you that I'm yours tomorrow, on the contrary I can promise you that I will not always be yours; but I can also promise you that if you're with me now you are more likely to find someone else later. In the language of business this is referred to as *employability*. We cannot guarantee permanent employment, but there are indications that if you join this project, you will be more likely to find another project somewhere else afterwards. Companies attract competent project workers by exhibiting their employability standards: the average time it takes for a person who leaves the company to be engaged somewhere else. In the project society the concept of security is changed from a matter of the same repeating itself to a matter of the probability of passage. More generally we may therefore speak of the *passability* of individuals.

If joining a project really increases passability, i.e. the security of a greater likelihood of passage, employers may go easy on other forms of remuneration. If the mere fact that you hook up with us will increase your chances in life, it would surely be a matter of overpayment if you also took a salary. Why don't you start here as an intern? Indeed it would tantamount to overpayment, if we were to guarantee that the project will come off at all. Why don't you freelance?

The freelance culture that emanates from projectual organisation works from organisations to the individual, but also from individual to organisation. Football clubs, for instance, are working hard to bind individuals to prevent them from joining projects elsewhere. The erosion of repetition and the consequent focus on the problem of passage also occurs between individuals, e.g. in private relationships, where leaving the other – to pass on and thereby leaving the other with a problem of passage – seems to have become an increasingly more acceptable possibility in the course of the twentieth century. The logic of the single life is slipping into the way in which individuals understand the overall condition of their lives – the project society – unfurling the passage within couplehood, if not as an actuality, then at least as a possibility. And the fact that people have to understand security as probability and the passage as a possible way out has undoubtedly had an impact on private relationships, friendships, kinships and professional relationships.

It is one thing that temporariness is the climate of the project society, its basic condition. It makes it possible to speak of temporariness as something natural or as a necessity, which causes demands for or expectations of predictability to appear as unreasonable or old-fashioned. Yet it is quite another matter if this basic condition may be exploited as a social technology.

What is a social technology? A social technology is an instrument with which one can manage and regulate social behaviour. Traffic lights are made up of scientific technology: the actual light signals. But apart from that, they also comprise a social technology: a regulation of traffic by means of temporal intervals, prohibition and permission – the shifting of red, yellow and green. The roundabout is another form of social technology, which also works according to prohibition and permission, but not by means of temporal regulations determined by a neutral body. The interlacement of roads is a third form of social technology.

The fact that temporariness may be exploited as a social technology means that people may be regulated by exploiting the fact that they know the project will terminate while not knowing what to do afterwards. 'Let's see what happens' leaves one with the impression that things will not continue regardless and, secondly, that everything is uncertain. We'll see about that later. In a manner of speaking, it no longer suffices for the individual to meet certain demands; everyone has to strive for overachievement in order to influence probability.

Temporariness is the basic element of insecurity to which we must add a number of other uncertainty factors produced by the kind of *uncertainties* described above: the fact that it is impossible to know how the project turns out, what a project is in the first place, who is part of the project, how the project is to progress (it has no time table), by which criteria it is to be evaluated, etc. The project society is a relation of the functions of temporariness, uncertainty, passage, project and connections.

Any factor that stresses the individual can be exploited in attempts to maximise results without the individual necessarily being aware that this is actually what is happening. If I insinuate that I might leave you, you will become all the more concerned about satisfying my needs. If we make it known that we do not know what our future needs will be, we provoke individuals to develop qualifications in all kinds of directions to prepare for any eventuality. If we refrain from making any demands that would provide the individual with an indication of when something is good enough, they will take excessive pains to do their very best in order to be able to pass. Stress factors may be multiplied as part of a managerial strategy by communicating sheer incapacity to anticipate the future.

I make no claims that this is something that improves people or projects in the long term, only that temporariness as a condition of contingency may be employed as a social technology between people. On the contrary, it is not hard to imagine that individuals would sometimes be capable of greater accomplishments if their passage was guaranteed. And if the project manager was seen as the one who would guarantee both the completion of the project and the passage of the individuals before the project finishes.

Without a doubt the exposure to the social technology of future-blindness may have severe human consequences. But since individuals are not circulating within closed spaces, any consequences are just sent on along with the individual.

Insecurity is engrafted into the general devolution of control to self-control in the project society. Whereas the disciplinarian society used to monitor people from a central point, e.g. a watchtower, surveillance is no longer necessary to the same extent. Why? Because it is in the individual's own interest to do things as well as possible with the aim of getting new projects. Controlling things from a central position is no longer as desirable as it used to be either. Why? Because controlling employees the way industrial workers used to be controlled only blocks their creativity and their keenness to experiment. Control has come to mean distrust. Subjecting people to control damages your relation to them, whether they be employees or boyfriends or girlfriends. Finally it is not even possible to control work the way it used to be. Why? Because it would require work to follow specifically planned processes by means of which it might be evaluated. In cases when one actually wants to control the project between its beginning and finalisation, one has to divide it into phases and specify certain aims for each of the phases. On the other hand, asking of a project that it arrive at particular stations at certain junctures only causes the projected to be directed a priori and then it begins to look more like a duty or an assignment. A project unfurls freely only if individuals are not controlled or assessed along the way.

The only thing that is to be controlled in the project society is self-control, i.e. it has to be checked if the individual has anything at stake in the project, if the individual *wants* to do this, is enthusiastic about it, desires it, if he or she wishes to develop certain qualifications as part of his or her own passage. If that is the case, the individual will do whatever it takes to do the job and it is not necessary to intervene. In contrast, a demotivated individual is one of the most dangerous things.

The transition to motivation-based management is particularly evident in the social services. Traditionally the social services would unfurl a space of rights and duties: citizens had a right to certain benefits if they would meet certain duties. The role of social workers was then to place the client according to an impartial assessment.

The transition of the social services to the project society takes place via a plan of action and a contract. Brought about by the insight that the bureaucratic machinery did not pay enough regard to the specific needs of the individual by simply placing individuals in different regulatory categories, the

1980s saw a gradual redirection of focus towards an increased concern with the specific situations of individuals. There is a parallel of this in the literature on organisation at the time in which the needs and feelings of the individual became objects of managerial attention. The new objective was to encourage clients to engage themselves in solving their own social problems – and gradually to make them responsible for the way in which these problems were dealt with. In order to make a client responsible one has to give him options and opportunities, he must be empowered. In the course of the 1980s the task of the social worker became one of informing and supporting the client, on the one hand, and, on the other, to motivate her to take responsibility for her own situation. A proper client must have a project. A project for her integration into society, her entry into the labour market or her exit from a criminal background. This involves a transition from one space to another: from a space unfurled by administered rights and duties to a projectual space unfurled by the individual. In this way the social worker turns into a project manager who specialises in passages: The aim is to get individuals to create projects they may pass onto.

It is no wonder if the social services look like the love of one's neighbour. The passage manager is the shepherd par excellence, and Christianity has more than 1500 years of experience in that kind of thing. In Western culture, which is more Christian than it is ready to admit to from a management perspective, draws heavily on the Christian cure of souls in anything that comes close to an interview on personal development and passage, from the civil services and private interviews with your employer on job satisfaction to coaching and project management.

What happens if you don't have a project? You demote the project manager to administrator. In order for the game to work everybody has to look at everybody else as engaged in and motivated for projects. The moment someone informs the job centre that he or she is not interested in finding a job, a spanner is thrown into the machinery. The moment you refer to your rights and duties, you won't get the same kind of support or be offered the kind of opportunities would if you decided to play the project game with the social services. To put it somewhat differently, you wouldn't get the kind of treatment you'd get if it wasn't possible to engage yourself in projects. As long as you give the expression that you want to unfold new spaces, you will not be folded into a fixed point – i.e. as long as you give the impression that you are already perfectly capable of functioning in the project society, you will avoid being treated as an inert body that only needs to be fed.

This somewhat exaggerated analysis is meant to shed some light on the fact that the project society's relation to rights is a rather precarious affair. There's no doubt that projectual individuals still risk facing the idea of rights as an organisational basis under certain circumstances – e.g. if they break the law. But rights as something that protect the individual do not appear to be all that protective anymore, because the crucial point is no longer that you are an individual but that you are able to negotiate. As administrators of rights are enjoined to assess special cases subjectively – and as their assessments bear increasingly upon the individual's personal involvement and enthusiasm rather than his or her objective case – it becomes increasingly undesirable for the individual to refer to her rights. If the consequence of referring to your rights is that the entire administration of your situation turns into a matter of a 'case' to be handled, it may very well be disadvantageous to demand your rights. Accordingly it has now become far more important for the individual to be able to pose as motivated, involved, affable, extrovert and keen to move on. The project society installs a kind of project normativity through which the idea of having projects becomes decisive for the kind of opportunities that are passed on to you. The legal system and administrative systems are not exempt from this.

7.

Connections in the Project Society

When speaking of human relationships as *relations*, individuals
are conceptualised as fixed entities that enter into connection
with each other within a fixed structure. Thus the structure of
space is seen as made up of a multiplicity of relations. A neighbour relation, for instance, is a connection to a person in the
space next to you, whereas a love relation may be a relation to
your neighbour's daughter, or someone else's daughter. Relations involve horizontal or vertical positions within a familiar
structure. To speak of interhuman contact in that way is better
suited for the disciplinarian society than the project society. In
the project society the being of the individual is not defined
by his or her position within a structure, it is unfurled by the
connections they make with each other within something that
is not already a coherent structure.

To the extent that we are now living in a projectual society,
which we aren't completely, relations are converted into connections. This does not mean that language keeps pace. For
example, all kinds of Internet forums whose purpose it is to
map and facilitate new connections between individuals and
to constitute the being of individuals as a profile among mul-
titudes, operate with a designation of these connections, and
the value of these connections, as 'friends', even if you cannot

expect the same from these connections as you can from your friends. Rather, it is all a matter of being online, connected – in short, interlinked. A relation is a tie within something that already coheres. A connection is something that is created between things that do not cohere.

If we take a look at the problems that are typically brought up by popular TV-series, they may give us an idea (though not an adequate one) of what is at stake for individuals nowadays. In the 1980s, series like *Dallas* and *Dynasty* were very popular. They depicted a vertical power struggle: How to reach the top, how to stay there, and how to bring others down? Series like that still exist. In Denmark we have *Matador* and *Krøniken*.

Apart from these family intrigues, another type of series was to gain ground particularly in the 1990s: series about friendships and singles. The advance of singles through series like *Ally McBeal* and *Sex and the City* points to a range of new problems in life. In these series everything does not revolve around gaining power, but around finding a husband. Problems of navigation dominate the picture, rather than struggles. Problems are horizontal rather than vertical. In these series women in particular, the glue of the disciplinary family, cast the parts of the ones who are to learn how to thrive in the project society. When *Sex and the City* starts with raising the problem of how a man has sex, it is not just about a woman's struggle for power against men. Rather, it is a question women ask themselves to find out how to flourish in life as a single.

If we cast brief glance at the history of feminism, it may be seen as divided into three phases. The initial phase at the beginning of the twentieth century was about creating a space for women in the first place by being acknowledged as individuals and as citizens. Women were enfranchised in Denmark in 1915, and in 1929 Virginia Woolf wrote *A Room of One's Own*. The second phase of feminism coincided with the revolt against traditional social structures in the 1960s and '70s. This phase was not only about the creation of a room of their own, but about leaving the room to fight for equality with men. This was a power struggle in which women were fighting to be equal with men – if not downright identical – on the one hand, and, on the other, for the recognition of a special feminine nature or womanliness. At times the two objectives would clash. In the third phase the issue is no longer oppression but expression. Now the demand of women being equal to do things is no longer a question of what they are deemed able to do or allowed to, it is about what the individual woman is capable of doing and therefore has to do. Consequently, the forces of conflict between men and women starts bending ahead in a reciprocal polygamous exertion. No one fears abuse anymore, now everybody wants to be abused.

The conditions of projectual man are exhibited in the type of TV-series that is about the lives of singles. The problems they depict can hardly be said to be typical of all singles, but the series testify to the fact that a new type of problems of connection and self-expression has become very exciting to watch, including the mum whose sex life has been washed out by the humdrum of family life. The representations of the project society arouse our curiosity exactly when they touch on the fractured interface between the disciplinary society and the project society.

The agonies and ecstasies of singles in making connections and unfurling their lives are most clearly exhibited in the TV-series *Sex and the City*. The mission of each of the four female main characters consists in mapping social connections in Manhattan in order to increase the success of their lives – and eventually to find a husband. An important task in this regard is to identify different types of men and to decode their logic in order to improve ways of getting on with them. While waiting for the family, a network of friends takes its place, which is also the case in a number of similar series from the 1990s (as spelled out in the title of the series *Friends*). This is a place one retreats to when projects terminate. The reason why the question of having sex the way men do is not only about how to achieve equality with men and how to unfold one's potential to a maximum, but also about navigating in a chaos of connections and expectations, is that passage has become a permanent condition of life. Living *en passant* has become normal, and even if the ambition of moving from single life into family life is still a major driving force, the passage is nevertheless a condition that is lauded in TV-series as well as in women's magazines and so-called chic-lit.

In the world shaped by disciplines, power was associated with position. Accordingly, social struggles were about establishing a position for oneself – just as the sociological analyses at the time were analyses of positions and relations (e.g. Pierre Bourdieu's sociology). If the passage has installed itself as a fundamental condition in the project society – and that is the claim that I make – this also reconfigures our view on human relationships. Interhuman contact ceases to be a matter of horizontal and vertical relations within a pregiven space. Instead collective spaces are opened by connections. As on the dance floor these connections may be established in movement, they may have various meanings and are never unrivalled. The only thing that is required is activity. The project is this activity.

Whereas in the disciplinary society people would arrange meetings, e.g. a rendezvous or a date, people in the project society make connections within the passage. The space of the project society is architecturally designed for meetings to take place everywhere, accordingly, not least in the passageways. The settings in the TV-series are moving out into public space.

The reason why sex is a predominant theme is not only because it fits well with the episodic composition of the shows. It also owes to the fact that transgression is part of the logic of the project society. A sexproject comprises a double attack on the twosomeness of the disciplinary society: It does not aim for repetition and it experiments with boundaries. These series are filled with sex – as long as it stays with the talking, mind you.

In *Sex and the City* four women range within the extremes

of the disciplinarily-minded Charlotte and the projectually-minded Samantha. The former dreams of the family and the latter of expanding herself as often and as variedly as possible without involving any feelings. The remaining two characters, Carrie and Miranda, are distributed between Charlotte and Samantha with each their peculiarities. The gist of the series is to derive a system from different experiences with different men. A typology of the various types of connection is unfurled, which is discussed by four different positions ranging from the disciplinary to the projectual woman. The following types of connection are played out: the meeting *en passant, one night stand, ugly sex, secret sex, the fuck buddy, the bootie call,* the affair, the date, the exclusive agreement, the boyfriends, the flatmates and marriage. The task is now to infer a number of rules of how to frequent the company of men within the different types of connection, how to establish the connections, how to administer them, how to communicate them and how to end them. Within another dimension of the series various types of sexual activity are problematised – e.g. anal sex, oral sex, the combination of anal and oral sex, the penetration of men, the use of dildos, etc. This list of problems is about what is desirable, in what way it is desirable, what men expect from you, how to establish this or how to avoid it. The various activities then combine with the various types of relations, raising questions of what one does with whom and when. E.g. what is acceptable after having spent a night together, a week, a month, a year?

The series tries to run through a mode of combination that

is supposed to trick the project society out of its secrets – in this case, the cunning logic of single life. It is pointed out that the ordinary spheres of *do's and don'ts* have disintegrated, which is why everything is possible in principle. Individuals may definitely unfurl themselves here! However, as they unfurl themselves the characters realise that everything is not possible after all, and that everything is not necessarily desirable either. In many ways this is the situation of the projectual individual in a nutshell: Everything is possible, but it is not possible to do just anything.

Single themes like the creation of connections, going online, going offline and the exploitation of connections are emblematic of the project society. The problem of being single in the disciplinarian society was different; as in Aristophanes' narrative in Plato's *Symposium* it was a question of finding one's missing half. The establishment of relations with the aim of repetition. The creation of connections has incorporated temporariness into its way of dealing with others, if not as something that is desirable then at least as something that is to be expected. Connections are ad hoc and do not involve any reciprocal obligations, accordingly. Connections have lost the kind of significance that applied to relations between positions, or the old kind of friendship. Relations still exist, as a foundation of projectual connections, but it is not in the nature of the project to establish connections that oblige individuals. The fact that the individuals of the project society are called friends within an Internet forum obliges no one. The fact that the number of phone numbers in my mobile phone keeps growing doesn't mean that I keep getting more actual friends. Or rather, if I think I do, the concept of friendship has to be redefined to incorporate the notion of temporariness.

What does it mean to change one's relations into connections? As Niel McCauley says in the movie *Heat,* it is all about not getting attached to anyone that you're not ready to leave in thirty seconds, if things start getting hot. In the project society it is all about placing your connections somewhere within an intermediary range: close enough to be able to make connections with people and sufficiently removed for them not to prevent you from entering new projects with other people. When relations have been changed into connections, they do not form a structure anymore, but a network. The creation of networks in the project society is partly about incorporating people you don't know into your network by attracting their attention and exchanging the necessary data, but it's also about converting the contacts with people you already know into network connections. That is, to keep them at a distance, yet close enough for them to range among your connections. A connection is like someone who is at sleep: you may wake her up whenever you need her, whenever you have a project.

Why did *networking* suddenly return as part of conference programmes? Because the network has become a legitimate way of co-ordinating and distributing goods. In fact it is not only legitimate, it has also turned into an altogether common and sensible way of connecting people – or rather, of getting them to connect and work something out. The bureaucratic machines of the disciplinarian society would co-ordinate individuals according to an overall plan. E.g. they would transfer an engineer to another department because he was needed there, or withdraw the midfielder a bit to strengthen the defence. In the project society such overall co-ordination has vanished; efforts are made to fertilize the ground in order for something to grow from below.

Up until well into the 1980s networks were still rather suspicious. They were associated with the mafia or underground movements. A network was something 'outside the system'. The difference now is not that networks have changed, but that the context networks enter into and take shape from have changed: the activity of networking now takes shape as temporary projects rather than a repetition of planned tasks. Likewise project management is about inciting and inviting individuals rather than commanding them.

As networks are gaining ground, descriptions of the nature of society as a society of networks also swell in number. These descriptions mostly build on biological models of explanation from the 1950s on that explain biological phenomena as systems of communication. E.g. the body is understood as one big communication system: Genes are codes, the white blood cells transport information, messages circulate and muscles discharge nerve signals. In addition to systems theory, cybernetics and communication theory, one comes across loans from chaos theory and theory of self-organisation and complexity theory – sometimes as theses of natural origin ('in the beginning was the network'), at other times as a phenomena induced by history. All these theories share a revaluation of relational attributes in preference to substantial attributes with communication theory – i.e. things obtain their value and capabilities from their networks. Transversal connections are emphasised rather than neighbourhood.

Organisation theories – which are rarely at the cutting edge when it comes to new thinking – follows suit. They draw pictures of weavings, of meshes, heddle eyes, knots, loops. Organisation is described as fluent, it consists of channels through which people are communicating. Or as a brain with synapses, with self-regulating and self-organising parts.

Network theories are more typical for our time than they are surprising. Still one may ask if these descriptions are not perfectly telling of our time, and if it isn't right to say that we are living in a network society rather than a project society? By emphasising connections they lose sight of three important aspects, though. Firstly, connections are nothing without activity; if no one was doing anything besides making connections, connections would not in themselves have any value. Evidently connections are created through activity, as in the example of dancing. Secondly, there is a tendency to overlook the fact that people have intentions, wills, desires, wishes and dreams, which they keep projecting, and that these wills and intentions are separated by gaps. As the saying goes, people have projects on behalf of others, but also on behalf of themselves. Thirdly, it is ignored that people keep thinking ahead. Humans open spaces and close them again. They open up time. Viewing society as a network may open our eyes to the significance of connections, but it does not render visible the fact that humans want to or have to do something else besides communication, or that they act as something other than communicating beings.

Yet, I haven't completely answered the question of why the network has returned to conference programmes. The reason why organisation from below has been able to challenge disciplinary, bureaucratic forms of organisation is that it is more flexible. The appearance of the network must be seen as part of a challenge. Discipline was brilliant at calculating and systematising things, at eliminating chance occurrences and repeating the same routines. What it couldn't do, among other things, was to transform itself.

E.g. the reason why the libero worked as a team trick in football as it was played in the 1970s was that a project worker was suddenly thrown into a disciplinary machinery. Suddenly there was a man in the middle of the defence who was free to be creative and to move all over the field. This kind of flexibility would confuse the teams that were capable only of thinking in terms of zones: the libero would move across zones. The reason why the Danish libero Morten Olsen forced a penalty against West Germany in the World Cup in Mexico in 1986 was that he suddenly tore himself loose and dribbled half a field while the German defence and midfielders were busy doing their duty.

Disciplinary machineries have great difficulty stemming this kind of flexibility.

Similarly it may be noted how companies in the course of the 1970s and 1980s began increasingly to challenge each other on the speed of readjustment, the renewal of products, or, as it was sometimes called, product innovation. In this context bureaucratic and top down forms of organisation are too heavy and slow. If every bit of change is to travel all the way up through a hierarchy of command to a central unit that makes a decision and sends back a message to a link lower in the chain, then the organisation's speed of readjustment is too slow. The demands or the tastes of the market have already changed again by the time the company gets around to the production stage. In order to prevent this, measures of conversion are enforced all the way down through the organisation, and in order for that to work, the competence of decision-making will have to follow. Self-organising teams or network-based organisations are put into practice. This is where descriptions of organisation as self-organising brains or bodies come into the picture, like chocolate box illustrations of the ideal of this form of organisation.

However, it is just as important that the option of inviting tenders for parts of the production is recognised as part of the answer when companies challenge each other on flexibility. Why? Because ownership of the means of production is no longer a strong point in and by itself, now and then it turns out to be a weakness. Readjustment is slow if one needs to include a change in the production of materialities in the process of trans-formation. If a company has old products in stock, they may become unsalable. It is better if others keep products in stock that we may be buying from – and that we leave it to others to possess the means of production, and place our orders with them. In the project society companies are always striving to shift all problems of inflexibility onto others in order to make themselves more flexible. This may apply to means of produc-tion and stocks, but it may also apply to time. To the extent that I can leave it to others to keep all kinds of things at my disposal, I will become all the more flexible myself. And that is why it is all a matter of keeping everybody at a networking distance, at an intermediary range. The reason why it is easy for the sailor to be away from home most of the year is not that he doesn't have a girl to return to, it is because he keeps a girl in every port.

The fact that the network is back on the conference program coincides with the fact that housing and jobs are distributed through networks. Furthermore, when jobs and housing are distributed through networks, they increasingly take form as projects and subletting. The generation of 1968 were fighting hierarchies through network-based forms of organisation, out-side the system. As said, my claim is that this struggle against discipline has come down to us as something else than it was intended to: as a project-based form of organisation. And the reason why the '68 generation now work as prime consultants in the project society is that they know its organisation from the inside.

I'm describing two kinds of intermixings here: First, what came of the showdown with hierarchy and discipline; that is, the project. Secondly, that the project almost always operates on top of, or enters into a connection with or relates to disciplinary forms of organisation that are still at work through spatial divisions, assessments, hierarchies, standardised work procedures, family patterns, etc. Contemporary society comprises a conflictual and complementary co-existence of these two ways of dealing with space, time, actions and relations. For instance, the women in *Sex and the City* want a kind of family in which it is still possible to live in a kind of single life mode – which is exactly what seems to be missing in a series that was to become popular a few years later, *Desperate Housewives*. Yet, co-existent forms of organisation need not only be in conflict, they may also be referring to each other, which is the case, for instance, when the word 'friend' is used on Internet portals that aim to establish and exhibit network connections.

In addition, neither project nor discipline can be said always to remain the same. Columbus' project was different from Carrie's projects in *Sex and the City* because the former did not relate to discipline at all. (And of course there are other differences). But discipline also changes in the project society. For instance, discipline no longer appears to us as orderly, but as old-fashioned. It may appear exotic to those who are fed up with project employment. Disciplinary organisation began as a central power expanding control. Now discipline may appear to offer a repetition just the way Mum used to cook it.

If passage is a problem because projects are temporary or do not repeat themselves, then the network is part of the solution. In the project society knowing someone who knows someone is an arrangement that creates security. The project society *re-nepoticises* what people used to be busy *de-nepoticising*. As the distribution of goods and projects depends less and less on formal qualifications but on networks, society becomes increasing mafiotic.

The project society is no Liberal dream. The Liberal dream of projects is not about networks but about the circulation of individuals and market decisions. In the project society there is no collective capital within which reciprocal exploitation may be determined and equalised. Exploitation within the project society is indeterminable and asymmetric.

In the project society market decisions are no longer crucial, although connections and projects may very well be bought and sold. Liberal criticism of hierarchies and excessive control may have kept in step with the 1968 revolt against the so-called injustice of the state, but the result was neither flip nor a free market economy, it was projectual organisation. The project society is one way in which the market may work, and, the other way round, the market is something that reaches into projects. But, as said, the project society is no Liberal dream.

Is the project society mafiotic? Yes, to a certain extent, but it does not have the pronounced hierarchies that characterise the mafia. The lines of connection in the project society are more inconstant than the family ties of the mafia. The project society oscillates between the liberal and the mafiotic, or, rather, it organises itself through both models of distribution in variable combinations.

Paradoxically, the project society does not only pull the individual towards others but also draws it towards itself. As the individual keeps passing from one project to another, the self is all that is carried along. The individual has no foundation in the form of something collectively shared. On the contrary, the individual constantly needs to plug onto a self – a self with a range of experiences, i.e. a portfolio of projects. Accordingly, it becomes important to draw attention to oneself, to consolidate oneself as a brand. Self-branding is a natural consequence of projectual organisation because the possibility of plugging on to something or someone depends on visibility. Hence, the project has to contain the signature of the self – your participation must show on the project – and the project has to brand the self – he was the one who took part in ...

When individuals are no longer tied together by formal types of organisation and distribution, but have to rely on the self as forming an independent mass that throws out projects, certain kinds of qualities are prioritised. It gives extrovert, inventive and confidence-inspiring people an advantage. Although the organisational structure of the project society is sometimes referred to as flat, we are not to imagine that it has ceased to be hierarchical. Its hierarchies have ceased to be formally visible, that's all. As the formal frames of the organisation disintegrate, they are succeeded by another kind of distribution. People often

imagine that the absence of laws, systems and order only leads
to the law of the jungle, i.e. that people are fighting each other
like animals within a chaos of cynicism. This is not the case.
The reason why the women in *Sex and the City* are so busy mapping men through typological depictions and a delineation of
rules is that even the asphalt jungle of Manhattan has an order
that requires advanced skills in sending off and interpreting
symbolic signals. The reason why we are so busy making sure
that our children acquire social skills at school is that social
skills have become a crucial parameter of competition in the
project society. You have to be able to establish connections,
to understand these connections, assess them, economise on
them, administer them and cut them off again.

The project society may be compared with a reception. You
have to circulate, avoid standing for too long with the ones you
know, make new acquaintances, advertise your accomplishments and your network, act energetic, extrovert and enthusiastic without appearing officious. You have to be someone
who is easy to connect with, i.e. you have to be attentive and
make yourself available. At the same time, you have to inspire
confidence in order that other people may dare to propose
projects with you without feeling that they are taking a risk.
Laughter and smiles are basic qualifications.

In his book *Discipline and Punish* Michel Foucault described
how the fight against the plague in the eighteenth century had
become a useful model for disciplinarian forms of organisation.
The plague was fought through a spatial division of cities and

careful regulation of movement and behaviour which caused cases of pest to be exposed, making it possible to isolate the disease and prevent it from spreading. Houses in which the plague was ravaging were exposed to disinfection, and gradually the sick were dying without contaminating others. Ideally an earlier principle of quarantine was employed, isolation, but now this principle was imported into the cities through the division of space, regulation, surveillance and control. This mode of control proved to be ideal for discipline. Gradually it became necessary to develop methods of control and surveillance that would not interrupt the work that discipline was organising – among other things, this was the reason why Bentham invented the famous Panopticon which is a type of prison in which the inmates cannot see that they are being surveyed and get to feel surveyed all the time as a consequence. Surveillance was silent; it would cause no interruption.

It appears to me that the way in which societies set about fighting AIDS, which appeared to be a new menacing epidemic towards the end of the twentieth century, was no coincidence. In order not to interrupt the activities of the project society it was important that people were not kept from connecting with each other. Isolation was out of the question, but still physical contact was to be prevented. How could you make sure that people would continue unabated to make contact with each other and enter into coupling projects of one kind or the other without touching each other or passing the disease on to each other? The solution was to recover an invention from the nineteenth century and dust it off: the condom. Condoms were marketed as moral reserve and associated with aesthetically dishy people. Suspecting one's bedfellow was not to be embarrassing; after all it was a matter of protecting both parties and therefore a solicitous act to reach for the French letters in the bedside drawer.

There are a lot of other reasons why precaution and safety with anything biological seems like common sense to us. However, it is worth noticing that the condom suits homo projectus very well, so to speak. In many ways the condom is the soul of the project society: It makes an endless number of connections possible without the consequences of actually touching. As far as the way in which the project society administers connections is concerned, it is a condom-society.

How do you get a project? Well, you may invent your own project and do it yourself or together with others. Or you may connect with someone who is in the middle of a project or about to launch one. In the disciplinarian society it was important not to get weeded out. In the project society it is important to be chosen. It is the logic of the schoolyard rather than the classroom.

The transition from the no of discipline to the yes of the project does not mean that everybody says yes to everything, but that people no longer say no in the same way. Silence is a no. The phone that doesn't ring or the e-mail that doesn't arrive. Rejection is the absence of connection. There is silence when a project terminates and this silence embodies the rejections of the project society. There are other types of missing connections, e.g. shelving or creating obstructions: It really sounds interesting, but I really can't come along because …

The reason why the psychologists of the project society are so busy teaching the individual to say no and how to back out may be due to the fact that projectual people have so great difficulties saying no. And why is that so difficult? Because a no is not a legitimate response within the climate of enthusiasm in which the competition for connections is played out; it isn't *comme il faut* to say no to something if nothing really prevents you from joining.

To have a network is a good basis for being chosen. The more you look like a socket with a lot of contacts the more attractive it is to connect with you. Another useful trick is passion and eagerness. A third parameter is to have looks. Since connections are temporary and are made in a flash, sensuous qualities are revaluated – there is simply no time for other impressions than the sensuous. The project society gives higher priority to aesthetics in its selections and this aestheticises people, things, relations and activities. Possibly, beautiful girls have always fared better than ugly ones. However, since the ugly girl is not allowed the time anymore to convince people of her inner beauty, and since the one we need right now is someone who will attract more connections to something that does not repeat itself, looks become a crucial parameter.

A fourth parameter is not to expect that the project is anything but temporary and that it involves no promises or prospects. Expecting control, guarantees and rules and stipulations is to prove yourself unsuitable for the project society. You may compete on the readiness to undertake risks: Not to expect any prospects or to do without a contract or payment, etc. Much of what the unions have been fighting for for more than a hundred year is now put up for auction through the underbidding that takes place as a central element of the competition for connections and projects in the project society. It isn't hard to imagine similar humiliations in the world of relationships, the tolerance of infidelity serving as attraction under the name of being 'free'.

Uncertainty is often smeared with a thin veneer of freedom to legitimise it, as the designation 'freelancer' seems to demonstrate. However, in the project society problems of inclusion and exclusion are not the prime issue, it is a matter of being connected or disconnected. Being connected, *branché*, as the French say, is a less determinable state of social belonging and certainly not a demand that may be raised collectively by a union of voices.

A fifth parameter is attached like a twin to the tolerance of relinquished guarantees: the tolerance of inflexibility. In the project society people compete for the greatest degree of flexibility. In that respect one may attract connections and projects by accepting inflexibility. It's alright that you don't know when exactly you're going to need me. Just say the word and I'll be there. This parameter may be identical with the absence of guarantees in the sense that a person is selling out on and creating flexibility by renouncing all guarantees.

The sixth parameter of competition is affiliated with this: the willingness to be abused. Since people would rather that others abuse them if the alternative is not being used for anything at all, and since abuse is taken as an opportunity for development, we have to make a distinction between abuse in the old sense of the word and abuse as it is understood in the project society. For instance, a person may join projects in which he or she gives up visibility – e.g. that you acquiesce in playing the guitar on a record while allowing the name of someone else to feature on the cover or play at the concerts as the official guitarist. But at times these two forms of exploitation – to be eager to be used and to be deprived of privileges unwillingly – join together nevertheless. By renouncing visibility, you keep plugging away and you keep getting contacts. Thus the elements of danger may compensate each other. Correspondingly, one may agree to join projects that offer no network at all in return for being engaged in something, perhaps even in something that one finds exciting.

The number of projects is a seventh parameter: a large number of projects shows that you are suited for projects and perhaps even that you are an attractive person to include in a project. The other way round, it is important to keep quiet if you don't have any projects (if possible at all), or, which is more common, to present your life itself in terms of projects. That may explain why we tend to ask our dinner partners what their projects are.

To remain in passage is an eight parameter: the greater the

capacity to keep passing on, the greater the possibility of carrying people before you in the passage to new projects. That is also why you should make a point of doing as many projects at the time as possible. The more transgressive your projects are, the better. The noise that you make as you crash into the disciplinary stratifications is a sign of talent in the project society. Not only is it exciting to take part in, it also supplies you with many different contacts. Every trick is doubly won in the sense that being active in projects gives you more contacts, increasing your chances of being invited for new projects *and* it causes you to appear as someone who is desirable to connect with. The one who dances a lot easily gets to dance even more.

When you have connections, it is important that you are also able to administer them. The first principle in this regard is visibility: to send off signals. This installs a *semiotics of connections* in which all your skills at the reception party are virtues. As said, it is a matter of inspiring confidence to make sure that others dare to connect with you despite the risks that are always involved in any project. It is about being enthusiastic and having something at stake. This way people feel reassured that you are not going to abscond. If you are capable of intimating something else in the conversations at the reception, underneath your obvious enthusiasm for the project, e.g. by giving the impression that the project contributes to your own passability (referred to e.g. as a CV or career), it will send off the signal that you have something on the line. Yet this card may be overplayed, causing the project to appear as something that just has to be done with.

· · ·   **III**   · · ·

Next, you have to rationalise on your contacts, i.e. you have to be economical in relation to your projects. It isn't possible to manage an endless number of connections, you have to park the passive ones properly in order that they may be resumed whenever you need it, you have to cultivate the ones that are potentially passable for more projects and close the ones that turn out to be blind alleys. As you don't say no in the project society, you have to develop a demeanour that helps you avoiding undesired connections. As said, you can allow things to peter out, you can put suggestions in cold storage, you can let the phone ring, refrain from answering, delay things or obstruct them.

Naturally this requires that you have knowledge of connections and projects. The semiotics and economy of connections must be supplemented with a *hermeneutics* of connections to prevent missing anything by the anticipation of 'what's in it'. The release of signs and the interpretation of signs interplay with each other; knowing that others interpret things in a certain way, you have to make your project look the way they like to see it. E.g. the finishing of a project may turn out to be more important than what it actually yields. Finishing your final dissertation may be more important than doing a fine dissertation if you want to make yourself attractive to projects in which speed is preferred to originality or professional skill.

One version of such ways of administering connections are to be found on the market in the form of PR, or in courses in selling oneself and networking. At the same time as the lonely hearts ads, through which singles used to put in for life mates,

CONNECTIONS IN THE PROJECT SOCIETY
· · ·

are versioned in the project society as dating sites for singles with another time frame, the temp agencies are growing big. If you don't have any contacts, you may buy them on the *contact market*. Part of this business consists in linking databases and suggesting matches of e.g. project makers and project purchasers, dance partners, sports mates, apartments, and the like.

In general it is a sign of attraction to have many projects. Yet a large number of projects may have an erosive effect on communication. On the dating sites on the Internet you may experience that everyone starts writing about how fed up they are with temporary connections. All of those who want a steady relationship and a couple of children in a few years communicate consistency, monogamy and ideas of permanence ... with a lot of people. The substance of connections changes when the number of connections is multiplied, even if the words are the same. Self-marketing may very well contribute to an increase in the number of projects, but it doesn't necessarily provide you with more security. You may come across the paradox that the accumulation of a great deal of small possibilities does not increase the overall possibility: In this case, that the power of a statement comes loose from the content of the sentence the moment it is communicated to a lot of people – just as nobody bothers to read e-mails that are sent round to a lot of people.

The temporariness of projects also has something to do with the temporariness of connections. Mixing with project requires that you understand that there is a quite wide spectrum between repetition and *en passant*. There is a wide range of connections between marriage and a fleeting encounter which relate more or less explicitly to different expectations of temporal duration: Connections with an explicit aim for permanence, e.g. an engagement ring. Connections with an unspecified duration but an implicit aim for permanence, e.g. a girlfriend or boyfriend. Connections with an unspecified duration and no implicit aim for permanence, e.g. an affair. Connections with an unspecified duration and an implicit aim for termination, e.g. a sustained relationship with an ex-boyfriend or ex-girlfriend. Connections with a specified duration, e.g. a holiday girlfriend or boyfriend. Connections that are in force and may be activated at separate points in time without any duration linking them together: all sorts of variations of having a lover. One of the reasons why *Sex and the City* is an apt representation of the project society is that it maps all of the variations of connections between *en passant* and *forever* as well as it exhibits the kind of semiotics of connections, the kind of hermeneutics of connections, the kind of connections economy and access to the connections market it takes to be a projectual person.

Sometimes it is impossible to communicate the nature and the status of the connections without changing or destroying the thing you want to communicate. Getting on in the project society is also a matter of knowing exactly when it is alright to speak out loud about the project society and when it is better to pretend as if you're not in the project society at all. Usually the latter is a good idea, but not always.

As the women in *Sex and the City* are busy making sense of

the logic of their own single culture, they often reach the conclusion that not everything is sayable, or that things will have
to be put differently from what they really are if you want to
achieve what you had in mind. If you want a permanent connection, it may be opportune not to let it show. This is the typical
plot of a classic comedy of love in which the woman thinks the
man does not want to marry, and the man thinks the woman
wants nothing but to marry, with the result that a reciprocal
playacting ensues in which the aim is to pretend that you want
what the other wants in order to obtain what you really want.
In the single series of the project society that kind of comedy
is rearranged as seriality, and the road to success is far longer.
In the first seasons of *Sex and the City* it is up for discussion
whether the event of being hurled out of the samsara of projectual life, out into marriage, will actually make you happy,
but gradually this series too assumes a romantic-disciplinary
form. The main issue here is communication, that you keep
abreast of the times, i.e. to communicate temporariness and
projectuality. Now the moral dilemma of the series is between
the desire to explore new things and to be acknowledged, on
the one hand, and the longing for security and family, on the
other. Accordingly, the introductory problem of 'how to have
sex like a man?' is redefined as a problem of 'how to live like a
single in a steady relationship?'. This is a problem that the individuals of the project society experience not only as something
imposed upon them from the outside, but as something that
they want: How to live like a projectual being within repetition?

8.

System and Style, Combination and Improvisation

I have touched upon a number of different transitions to the project society: from the coded programs of couple dancing to the unfurling of the self in the energy dance, from the bending of nature by the industrial sport to the surfer riding the forces of nature, from field-position football to the football of movement, from the lonely ones to the lives of singles, from the closed office doors and classrooms to the passageways and readjustable walls, from the pedagogy of training to the development of individual qualifications, from the rights and duties of the social services to self-initiated social service, from bureaucracies and plans to the business of calling for tenders. As far as I can see, all of these transitions represent different manifestations of something that may be understood as but one singular transition. The driving force of this singular transition cannot be located within one of its different manifestations, which goes to show that the transition takes place in all of these areas simultaneously. Likewise disciplinary organisation has proved to be strong and weak in similar ways within all of the areas. Of course this does not exclude the possibility of reciprocal inspirations – certainly not as long as the different areas are blended in projects.

All of these activities may be counted among the things and occurrences that are commonly referred to as society. They are all common, peaceful functions that have been transformed. In contrast, *war* is often considered to be a function that lies outside society. It is considered to be a state of exception in which other ploys, other rules and other laws apply – if any at all. Nevertheless, the logic of the project society also makes itself felt in war – because war is, in fact, also part of the society that is turning into a project society.

Conventional armies operate from a territory and are structured like a bureaucracy in the form of a pyramid with a few leaders on top, a number of officers and a large number of private soldiers at the bottom. From above it looks like a star with a centre from which orders run to the points which execute the orders and report back to the centre.

In contrast a guerrilla army has no territories and no safe zones. As a rule it operates on the territory of the enemy. Guerrilla armies are organised polycentrically, i.e. as a lot of cells that are not hierarchically connected, but operate autonomously. Conventional warfare used to be about defeating the rival army by decapitation: When the top of the enemy's body was cut off, the rest would bleed to death. Yet it was often necessary to fight some of the limbs to reach the head. A guerrilla army has many heads which is why it cannot be fought the same way. It is protected by its organisational form, precisely as in the kind of football in which all of the players move around the entire field. A guerrilla army must be fought cell by cell, and still it is impossible to roll up its network. That is exactly why the use of napalm during the Vietnam War was a logical choice: If you couldn't strike the head, you had to do something to the environment.

Hitchcock's *The Birds* from 1963 shows that there is something which is even harder to fight than a many-headed monster: a swarm. Different groups like Al Qaeda, Abu Sayyaf, Jemah Islamiah, The Tamil Tigers, Combat 18, PKK, the Chechen militia, Ku Klux Klan, Shining Path, Hamas, Islamic Jihad, PFLP and Hizbollah all represent an organisation of manpower that is almost flat and extremely flexible. They are all ad hoc-groups rallying round a project, e.g. a terror project. They have no territory but they are highly mobile. Like companies they operate with a dual relationship to names: On the one hand, a name may be replaced. On the other hand, a name may be deployed like a brand. An act of terror in some country may be claimed to be e.g. an Al Qaeda-attack. Attacks may be supported or sponsored by networks.

It would be foolish to fight a swarm of bees with a flyswatter. In wars against guerrillas, armies have the option of fighting the environment. But this form of environmental destruction is not a feasible strategy against groups that never keep to any particular area and may be present everywhere. This way most of the world would have to be destroyed as the network is all over the place in civilian populations which is also where it emanates from. What to do then? First of all, if networks arise from among civilians, measures have to be taken against civil-

· · · 118 · · ·

ian populations. Either by waging war against the population in question, or by making war as *nation building*, i.e. you weaken a country and build it up again to convert the population, e.g. accustoming the people to democracy or turning them into consumers. Secondly, knowing that networks communicate is a cause for taking action against communication rather than volume, e.g. by fortifying intelligence to intercept communication and start circulations of communication. Thirdly, the military powers have to transform themselves into networks up to a point in order to adjust to the networks they are up against. This is possible only if some of the decision-making power is delegated to the common soldier, who now has to be retrained as a mid-level manager and communication officer. This is not because the network is more equitable, but because the belligerent powers are forced to outbid the disciplinarian model of organisation with more flexible forms that are capable of handling a greater degree of contingency and keep their end up at the communicative level. In this way new types of armies are emerging which are supposed to be able to operate as a combination of central control and autonomous networks – just as the modern football of movement can be said to be a mixture of flexible Total Football with a greater focus on movement and field-position football operating in accordance with the aim of controlling spaces.

Discipline has lost the command of space. To extend that it was no longer possible to structure time by spatial means, it was no longer possible to predetermine actions in time either.

Conversely, it was through activity, actions, that the project took over the command of time and space. By basing the project on activity, activity became the basis of time and space. For example. Ideally, a striker in Total Football is no longer someone who is playing within a certain, demarcated space of the field and has certain duties, any player turns into a striker the moment he or she takes possession of the ball and creates something with it.

Disciplinary organisation was brilliant at eliminating uncertainty by standardising activities, fixing them in time and space and bringing them to pass off according to a program. In the disciplinarian society you would run through a sequence and combine sequences. *The transition to the project society involves a transition from combinatory variants to improvisation.* The dancer no longer repeats a program, but improvises a unique expression. There are in-betweens in this transition. For example, what people have in mind when they refer to the Tango as a dance of improvisation is improvisation as a combination of variants: It is a matter of diversifying a range of regular figures, dismantling them and putting them back together again to form a dance that cannot be described as a repetition of a sequential program, but as an improvised variation of combinations – it may be compared with the way in which you can improvise different figures with a box of toy bricks.

The prime duties of the disciplinary mode of organisation were to eliminate coincidence and to optimise outcomes through sub-optimisations in relation to an overall plan. The weakness of discipline was that it was incapable of exploiting coincidences by incorporating them. The strength of the project is that the lack of a plan allows it to bide its time: to see the coming and going of chance occurrences and only then decide what steps to take.

The project challenges disciplinary organisation on its weakest points: Apart from the exploitation of contingency, these are: sensitivity, flexibility and the speed of readjustment. Disciplinary government does not pay any regard to the individuality of its object. For example, it makes plans for what children are to learn in the third class; it does not arrange its programs according the abilities of individuals or what they feel like doing. The project management does. Its purpose is to get the individual to express himself or herself. It is sensitive to customers, sensitive to pupils, sensitive to clients, sensitive to the individual person. It always changes with its object. The project need not take any claims for consistency into consideration because it never has to repeat itself. That is why one cannot count on a project in the future. But it is flexible, and it readjusts according to the needs of any specific situation at great speed.

The project challenges discipline on flexibility. Fitness clubs reflect this situation very well. Joining a sports club that allows its members to do sports only at a scheduled time has a restrictive influence on people who are increasingly getting used to arranging things on very short notice. Instead people prefer to join gyms or clubs where they may exercise at variable times of the day (and night) without notice. Moreover, the body movements within these clubs reflect the way in which discipline and flexibility coexist. While some people are working on their muscular strength by bending the forces of nature, other people are working on flexibility in the yoga room. The ability of the yogic body to stretch, curl and flex is a future-oriented counterpart to the project worker, whereas the big heavy strong body looks increasingly like the plated armour of the industrial society.

Discipline and project do not merely coexist. The project works in relation to, by virtue of, on top of and in connection with earlier social and organisational forms, including, especially, what I have comprised under a singular name: the disciplinarian society. In fact the disciplinarian society forms the basis of the project, its kindling force.

As illustrated, the disciplinarian society has many characteristics. One is the security it provides by guaranteeing individuals that they can rely on the repetition of the same, i.e. that the present is permanent. But in the last resort, permanence is sustained only by repetition, the way ladies with 'permanent' waves have to have them 'permed' at the hairdresser's at regular intervals.

The disciplinary world may work as a kindling force in relation to the project society in at least three ways. First: The driving force of the project is to *transgress* the barriers that the disciplinary society has established. E.g. people are doing cross-disciplinary projects. Secondly: The project may involve a *promise* of permanence. Individual projects are established with the aim of finally getting hurled out of the project way of life. People may take the offer of an internship with a view to permanent employment. Single life is fuelled by both of these ways of relating to discipline: as promiscuity and the family dream. Finally, and thirdly, the system of the project may be operating under the pretext of being disciplinarian. The way in which this works is by presenting the project as an *exception*. Gradually, as the exceptions keep repeating themselves, the exception installs itself as a permanent condition, but without the security of the disciplinary society. For example, the designation 'substitute' or 'temp' is used more and more without any other employee actually being replaced, just as other names for exceptions are becoming widely used.

It is only fair to ask if project living doesn't seem to involve a lot of repetition, if it isn't felt that way by projectual individuals. E.g. the single who will never be at rest in a steady relationship seems to be repeating the same pattern over and over again. Her increasingly skilful ways of handling the unknown have become so wonted that the unfamiliar look increasingly familiar. Without a doubt there is a degree of repetition in projects, but the repetition of projects differs from the repetition of discipline in two ways.

First of all, the repetition of a project is not a planned repetition, but a repetition through variation in the sense that the project is unfurled in ways that are generated by chance events and the incorporation of these chance events. Accordingly, the repetition of projects may be described as continuity through variation rather than a repetition of the same – what is at issue is a *style* rather than a program. A free kick combination is a program. It doesn't add up to a style of playing. Naturally there are elements of repetition in a style of playing, but they will never amount to a sequence or automatism. The project way of life is a style.

Secondly: The kind of continuity through variation that is sometimes brought about by the sheer number of projects pertains to the kind of disciplinarian repetition in which variation is not deliberately included as an objective (whenever we try to repeat something a degree of variation is inescapable). To stay with the example of the single: Repetitive dating with new men relates to the disciplinarian repetition of marriage, e.g. as a desire to terminate the former type of repetition (i.e. by getting married) or as a desire to sustain it (i.e. making sure to keep things at a projectual level by considering the relation as something that has to come to an end at some point).

Finally it must be added that project and discipline are modes of life that a person may move in and out of. If a player is sent off in a football match, his team will often give up some of their creative ambitions and fall back on prearranged duties. Similarly, a person may move back and forth between different types of jobs: between rather systematised types of jobs and more open projects with a different kind of expectation to the outcome. The same goes for living arrangements, ways of dancing and types of administration. Whenever you lose your partner, the music changes or a client happens to demand being put under administration, that's when you may change your style. In that sense, discipline, like the project, is not only a system of organisation, it is also a style that may be employed in handling the occurrences of unforeseen events.

9.

Being Human in the Project Society

The twentieth century witnessed how the project society was slowly leaking out from the chinks of the disciplinary society. Psychology came into the world and brought about various forms of therapy that were to stem or neutralise the nervous affections that people were developing as a consequence of the emergence of different types of societies. New types of diagnoses bear witness to new types of difficulties of being human. As new conditions were gradually embedded in individuals, they were described by the great European writers. Apart from diagnoses, literature offers some of the best eye-level testimonies to the way in which the conditions of homo projectus took shape bit by bit.

Franz Kafka was one of the writers who at an early stage identified the crisis of the individual as caused by a crisis of collective institutions. To Kafka the problem was that the law of society's institutions was too weak, which is why his characters keep turning to a court of law or a father to receive a sentence they cannot have. In *The Trial* from 1925 Joseph K is the one who stands accused. Throughout the entire novel he tries to find out what he is accused of in order to get his sentence or acquittal. He goes to see the 'Painter' who tells him that he may choose between two solutions: ostensible acquittal and postponement. None of them acquits the individual *res judicata*. If he chooses ostensible acquittal, the case will be tried before a judge who is empowered to acquit the accused temporarily but cannot pronounce a definite verdict of not guilty. K will then be acquitted by the court until the day he is arrested and put under trial again. The other option is postponement. The case will be constantly pushed around between a number of judges, making sure that it will never proceed beyond this primary stage. The absence of acquittal leaves the individual with the choice between, on the one hand, a life of pretence and fear – pretending to be free while constantly fearing the loss of freedom – and, on the other hand, a life in which freedom has to be perpetually re-ensured by pushing the problem around.

Kafka captures the kind of anxiety or unease that character-ises people in the project society. They have to live without any definitive confirmations, all they have are choices between dif-ferent kinds of temporariness – milk or the ice floe: One option is to enter into connections that appear to be lasting – e.g. jobs in which tasks keep repeating themselves – but the creeping sensation of getting stuck to the pan will set in sooner or later, and then the projectual individual will have to set out. Besides, people all around you keep leaving and breaking up, which is why interchangeability will always be a condition anyhow. The other option is to join projects that run out as time goes by. In that case you have to keep looking for new ice floes to jump onto when the one beneath you begins to melt.

Kafka heralded the kind of *inconclusiveness* that characterises the project society. You'll never reach a conclusion, you'll never finish. But his characters are still dreaming of closures and con-clusions in the form of a final examination, inquiry or verdict. But they will never reach any such closure. In the project society this inconclusiveness is a fundamental condition, i.e. not only are the criteria of a final decision or judgement unknown, the formation of such criteria is perpetually postponed.

This has something to do with the fact that the criteria of assessment are no longer given in advance of the activity that one would like to get an assessment of. Any criteria of assessment are continually reshaped by the project-activity, by new initiatives and by the emergence, or possible emergence, of other projects.

In the old school, assessment was based on the quality of the performance in question, i.e. the extent to which a performance would agree with a predetermined truth, answer or ideal. In the project society the crucial thing is more a matter of *what* is produced.

If projectual people are not evaluated on the basis of whether they live up to predetermined criteria, if they are not evaluated on the basis of whether they have made any mistakes or violated any rules or done their job well, how, then, are they evaluated? Any notion of the good project is not determined in terms of the extent to which it agrees with any standards, but in terms of originality and uniqueness. The projectual individual is not appraised in terms of obedience and dutifulness, but initiative. What did you create, what did you initiate? The clever child is no longer the one who can write an unflawed assignment according to some standard or key, it's the one who comes up with the most exciting projects. For this purpose there is no project manual, except the recommendation of transgressing disciplinary boundaries, which itself appears to have become rather unoriginal by now if it has no other purpose than transgression.

Naturally it takes certain skills to effect a project, but it also takes skills to deviate from a norm. On the one hand, project people have to get used to the fact that it is not only their skills that are subject to evaluation, but also their creations, and, on the other hand, they have to get used to the fact that no one knows what the criteria of evaluation are. Accordingly, inventiveness, transgression and deviation from disciplinary rules have become valuable skills, but so has the ability to endure the state of not knowing – the ability not to panic or get stressed about the fact that selection always keeps you waiting.

Kafka was a master at describing the transitional phase that threw the disciplinarian institutions into a state of crisis, but he was still thinking in terms of trials and judgement, i.e. the no. In the project society it is not judgement but the criteria of positive selection that remain deferred. And are deferred once more. Of course variation would creep in in the disciplinarian society, but the parameters of judgment and selection were always known. In Denmark it was uncertain how high your marks were supposed to be to be admitted at the university, e.g. to study medicine or economics, but you knew that everything depended on your marks. In the project society the very parameters judgment and selection are unknown. No one knows who's going to be asked to join the next project because the project hasn't been invented yet.

This kind of permanent deferment, in which nobody knows, results in a general pursuit of the immediate which often takes the form of an aestheticisation. The Kierkegaardian ethicist makes a choice, and he chooses himself through repetition. To marry is to choose a life with this man or this woman over and over again, and to commit to this choice. But when the conditions for the repetition have come to an end – when it has become impossible to believe that you'll be able to stay together for the rest of your lives as a consequence of the conditions of the project having become prevalent – then aesthetic valuations come to appear more sensible. If I cannot know what is to come, I might just as well choose what feels good right now. We adapt ourselves to ad hoc-solutions because the mode of repetition is unrealistic or undesirable. That's why homo projectus is an aesthete.

The uncertainty of the future establishes itself like a climate in the project society. The fact that the significance or the quality of a project are impossible to know means that a criteria like 'good enough' is impossible too. Everything in the project society is possible, but you are not capable of doing just anything. This may throw the projectual individual into a permanent feeling of insufficiency, if he or she still expects to get things done or feel secure in the old sense of the word.

I believe that the projectual organisation is a basic structural ingredient of a whole range of new pathologies like depression and stress. These pathologies are exacerbated by a society in which security cannot be based on repetition and people cannot know what is good enough or when they may think of themselves as adequately or sufficiently practised. Instead people carry around with their portfolios of projects and a bunch of qualifications they may develop indefinitely. In the same breath it is important to emphasise that the liberation from repetition is also makes a far more varied life possible with all kinds of different and overlapping projects. In this selfsame climate, in which all is possible but you cannot do everything, this is where individuals are both enthused by projects and breaking down all by themselves. Such atomised fates – people in the middle of ceaseless transgressions without the form of law (ceaseless transgressions losing steam) – are what the French writer Michel Houellebecq described towards the end of the 1990s as *Elementary Particles*.

The project society puts individuals in a situation in which they have to *want to* and have to *feel like* doing the things they do, and they have to be able to live with the fact that they *cannot know* whether their efforts are ever good enough. At the same time as everything is possible, because the project is a projection into the future whose virtue it is not to acknowledge any limits, then it is still not possible to do just anything. Individuals are constantly faced with their own *insufficiencies*: the possibilities that never came off. People used to be able to say that something was not possible because it was prohibited or impossible to carry through because of the rules on the area, but when there are no rules, when you are to invent your own rules, the failure of any attempt is suddenly ascribable only to the individual's own abilities.

At the beginning of this book I said that the projectual individual in Kierkegaard's terms, the project maker, was likely to be driven to despair by the infinity of possibilities, i.e. by the want of necessities. Projecting people are driven into despair because the project society offers no necessities. Projecting people come across no boundaries or limits, only enthusiasm and initiative. As a consequence, their only option, if they want to get on in the project society, is a headlong drive into the despair of possibilities. While constantly urged to think of new possibilities, they are left to stand alone with the feeling of insufficiency as most of all of these things come to nothing anyway.

Three additional conditions are attached to the four conditions I have mentioned above – inconclusiveness, expectations of passionate dedication, lack of knowledge and insufficiency – which make the situation of the individual very precarious. The individual who has connections is always alone. He or she may very well be joining other individuals in projects, but engaging in new projects is but a game of *individual fates*. There's room for more than one on the ice floe, but the search for new ice floes is an individual matter, and the results an individual matter of personal success or tragedy. All of this takes place in a state in which *temporariness* has consolidated like a climate, i.e. in which activities are carried out knowing that they have to end as well as any foundation has been replaced by ad hoc-situations. Finally it is not to be forgotten that disciplinary *valuations and expectations* are still in operation, pressurising the individual – wins in football, surplus on the bottom line, passed exams, payment on time, or whatever it may be. The individual must make sure to satisfy a whole range of demands while at the same time it has to invent what is in demand yet still unknown. What the individual cannot know is how significant or insignificant assessments and exams actually are. In that respect, judges and evaluators have become increasingly invalid. It may very well be that it is obligatory to pass a certain exam, for instance, but the question of whether your papers will ever make a difference cannot be answered. Proficiency in a subject no longer suffices. To get a job after your studies, you also have to have experience from student jobs, and interests and hobbies that you passionately devote yourself to may turn out to be just as decisive. But nobody knows.

The complexity and confusion of the situation has several consequences. First of all, actual judgement turns into a matter of *jugement*. People guesstimate. Whether you are deemed competent or not depends on a range of other than objective criteria, not least including appearance, willpower, zeal, drive and social skills. To make legal demands is *Spielverderberei* in the project society.

Secondly, it is by no means all who experience this confused situation as disagreeable. Teaching yourself to live like a projectual being also means to be able to come to terms with the idea that the only sure thing is that which may be seized in the moment, as nothing can be extended into the future. In return, aesthetic criteria become all the more relevant, because fleeting appearances is all you can rely on. The question of whether a person, a situation, a place is beautiful, yummy and appetising has become more relevant than the question of whether it is suitable as the object of a life, a repetition, a place to live. In turn, this has repercussions on the choice of the qualities individuals strive to foster within themselves.

Finally, in the third place, the transition from disciplinarian order to projectuality involves a change in the mental illnesses we are developing. I am well aware that mental sufferings are caused by a wide range of physiological and biological reasons, and I'm also aware of the fact that the variability of mental illnesses is also ascribable to the chequered career of categorisations and diagnoses. Even so, it is possible to identify certain changes that reflect the demands that are made on the individual by the different forms of social organisation and intercourse that I have sketched.

The disciplinarian society tended to develop a range of perversions which were either entirely undisciplined or entirely over-disciplined. Sometimes, when the disciplinary society was shushing its subjects, they would burst into noisy resistance. Either in the form of hysteria, which cries out all of those things that are not allowed into the open, or strikes, mutinies or riots, the masses gathering to tumble over the bars and barriers of society. Other than the noise, there is the neurosis: the incorporation of self-discipline and self-surveillance as a result of overdisciplining.

The project society does not shush people, it communicates. The yes, enthusiasm for the project, connections are communicated everywhere. The perversion of the project society is not hysteria, but depression. In the project society you can be anything but depressed: introvert, sociophobic, despondent, tired, not feeling like anything and indifferent or downright sad. Depression is: not to feel like doing any projects. Another kind of affliction that is produced by the conditions of the project society is stress. Interestingly, stress is not only caused by the load of responsibilities, but by uncertainty, temporariness and feelings of insufficiency: Is this alright, is it good enough? What's supposed to happen afterwards? What's the best thing to do now? Such worries of insufficiency, which are structurally generated, wear out the projectual individual.

So, breakdowns in the project society are not collective, like a strike, but individual. And they are quiet. Amidst the hum of voices and all the chinking of white wine glasses at the reception party, one may draw back from the conversation and become very quiet. This silence is not the silent no of the others, but your own no, your own lack of interest, your own lack of energy to open new spaces. This is where the dancing stops. Not because the music stops or the party ends, but because you are too done up to pedal the dynamo that gives out the light of your enthusiasm.

It is important that you remind yourself of three things. First, that this condition is structurally generated, i.e. that it is caused by a number of circumstances that are beyond the control of the projectual individual. Secondly, that the projectual way of life is a far more exciting way of living to many people, as opposed to a life tied to repetitions and routines. It is often possible to make the things you want to do doable. Thirdly, the upsetting effects of the indecisiveness brought about by the project society are not omnipotent. It is still possible to exploit the mixtures of definite bounds and projects that you come across – or to keep on to something while pursuing projects on other fronts. It is still possible to attend one's duties or learn specific dance steps by heart while developing one's own style of playing or dancing. Although the security produced by repetition is no longer supposed to be possible, it is still possible to increase the likelihood of certain passages. The project society is characterised precisely by the opportunity of the individual to do so much more now than before; it is no longer necessary to hunt up institutional spaces to be able to do certain things, anybody may open his or her own space of activity. So much more becomes possible this way, it just doesn't come with the same degree of security.

The old, hackneyed question of whether things are deteriorating or in a state of decline is getting impatient. I haven't answered that question. I've only tried to answer the question if the order of old has been replaced by chaos. Hopefully I have made it clear that the social is not disorganised just because it looks disorganised. But the question of whether the world has become a worse place to be cannot be answered in the same way. I prefer to return the question: worse for whom? For the quiet girl? Yes. For the one who is surfing around, no, not necessarily. It is a little like asking if the possibility of dissolving a marriage is good or bad for all people. It is good for some people and bad for others. But it goes for all that the condition of temporariness is something they are going to have to deal with in one way or another.

In his book *The Gay Science* Nietzsche proposes a quality test to his reader. The test is supposed to test the quality of existence: How would you feel if a demon came up to you and whispered into your ear that whatever you are going through now is something that you have to go through over and over again? If life without repetition is unbearably light, as Milan Kundera demonstrated in his love story *The Unbearable Lightness of Being*, the question of whether you *want* the things you are doing now to repeat themselves may be an offer of weight or gravity in life. The thought of inevitable repetition makes every little trivial event significant. And if you are terrified by the thought of a demon stealing upon you to whisper a couple of home truths like that into your ear, it pretty much seems as if there's a thing or two you need to change in your life, is what Nietzsche seems to suggest.

Similarly a litmus test could be performed on the existential pH-value of the projectual being: How would you feel if you were told that none of the things that you are doing are repeatable, including the connections you make? What would you do about your choices? People would take differently to such intelligence. Some would take comfort in it, others would find it disturbing. But it remains a universal condition that in spite of the fact that many areas of life are taking place within a space and time that has been stretched out by rules that are meant to facilitate repetition, the project as a form and as a climate is continually gaining ground in more and more areas of life, which causes one's fitness for the project society to depend on the ability to endure the idea that nothing is supposed to repeat itself. How do you feel, project man, about the thought that a demon is going to whisper into your ear that everything is temporary and that nothing is going to repeat itself?

Space was fixed by discipline, and its opponent was movement. There is no opposition or resistance in the project society, only individual collapses. This has to do with the fact that the principle of government is no longer training or modelling or moulding, but development. Formerly, when the labour force or the power of mathematics or desire or any other force was to be exploited, it was fitted into a cast or mould. Now people enter into relations of exploitation instead, in which they express themeselves. A project involves an attempt to cause exploitation and expression to coincide. The project is then to create the basis of a new project. However, there are no explicitable conflicts of interests within the coincidence of exploitation and expression, as I put it earlier, there are no opposing vectors, they are all bending ahead. Whereas discipline used to fix things, the project moves things. You cannot create movement in the form of resistance; at most you may shoot yourself in the foot by standing still. And be still.

And yet there is opposition and resistance in the project society. The huge demonstrations against environmental damage and capitalism that the world presently carries the weight of are organised like terror networks. Unlike the trade unions they do not operate through a mass of people who have surrendered their right to negotiation to a central unit which then pressurises an opponent in a conflict of interests. They are ad hoc-demonstrations in which a network has emerged from connections, gathering for a single demonstration-project only to separate again afterwards. The trade unions were made up of relations, creating a solid colossus with the power of exerting pressure. A single touch in any small spot could start up the entire machinery, open the strike fund, etc. The network does not have the power to exert the same kind of pressure; it isn't built up in a continuous fashion, but by new projects. In the project society people do not think in terms of foundations, but springboards. And that is one of the great weaknesses of the project society.

What would an opposition to the project society look like? Collective efforts would have to create an oppositional foundation. A foundation of what? A foundation of, or at least an element of security during the passage. Politically, it is hard to imagine that it would be possible to agree upon more stable conditions during the passage between partners in the lives of singles, whereas the creation of a foundation that makes it possible to endure the flexible organisation of the labour market seems to fall within the purview of politics. In the case that the objective is not to ban or abolish the project society, opposition would be a matter of creating foundations on which projects could take place. When a delegation of representatives of the French government visited Denmark in 2005 to examine why the Danish economy was not marked by the slump the rest of Western Europe was going through and a proportionally rising unemployment rate, emphasis was given to the flexible labour market in Denmark. Yet it was ambiguous, and it still is, whether the Danish labour market in this way was to be seen as exemplary in succeeding once again in meeting the demands of flexibility and suppleness, rendering the conditions of the individual still more precarious, or, the other way round, if the Danish labour market had managed to take care of the precarious conditions of the European economy by preserving an unemployment system in contradistinction to other European countries. However that may be, it goes to show that the creation of safety and security in the project society it is not only individually reassuring, but also collectively lucrative. To guarantee the passage of everybody may be an impossible task on a collective level, but surely it isn't impossible to guarantee the security of people in-between projects. One may think that a movement in the direction of some sort of basic income would be the most logical response to the project society, but this doesn't appear to be a widespread conclusion.

Yet this would not eliminate the logic of the project society either. The fact that people actually want to engage in all kinds of projects demonstrates that we shouldn't wish for things we cannot do anyway: to do away with the project society once and for all. Instead one may wish for the exploitation of uncertainty in the form of social technologies to end.

Challenging the conditions of the project society may also take the form of creating something. To safeguard oneself and others against the kind of uncertainty the passage entails long before a project expires. In other words, to deal with indeterminateness by means of determinateness. It may very well be that man is the as of yet undetermined animal, as Nietzsche said, and that we are deemed always to live with projects, as Sartre maintained. However, in a condition like that there is still a great difference between wanting to do everything, to say yes to everything without being able to make up one's mind, and then wanting to do something in particular. If no attempts are made also to close spaces in the pursuit of this uncertainty and the act of grafting one's own condition of uncertainty onto that of others, flexibility and freedom of movement may very well degenerate into situations in which one may feel like a fox in a chicken run without a fence. At the end of the day, even the projectual individual is aware that the one who wants something in particular is someone who is worth projecting with.

Kafka pointed out the invisibility of boundaries and conflicts. I plead guilty, I have overstepped a line I don't know, but

I cannot be convicted. Instead Joseph K had to try to choose between different ways of balancing his guilt. The transition to the project society involves a transition from boundary to balancing. In the disciplinarian society certain activities would belong to working life, others to family life, others to holidays and leisure, others to friendship and yet others to other social institutions. The sense of things getting mixed up as they are turning into projects creates problems of balancing for the individual. Rather than stumbling upon boundaries it stumbles on imbalances. Individuals have to know how to balance things – e.g. how to strike a work-life-balance, as it is sometimes put so inelegantly. These problems of balancing are created by the project's levelling of disciplinary spaces. In the project society, keeping things apart is not where it's at; everything is a matter of balancing these levelled spaces, to stay poised on the levelled spaces projects are constituted by. This exhausts you.

Kafka's books thematise what Freud had already figured out: that boundaries and conflicts are important for the ability to constitute a self. To Freud life was a high drama of guilt. In the disciplinarian society a successful individual was an obedient individual. The kind of individual who would stay out of any conflict with authorities.

In the project society boundaries seem difficult to spot for the wealth of possibilities. A successful project person is not obedient; he or she takes the initiative, connects and disconnects. Because everything is possible. And yet every projectual man or woman will come to realise that he or she isn't able to do just anything. If you never fall upon limits of the possible, you risk collapsing from exhaustion.

Depression spreads as the project society spreads and the disciplinary society fades out of sight. The first diagnoses of depression appeared towards the end of the 1940s and the number exploded already in the 1970s. To begin with, psychiatrists recognised depression as neurosis: as a conflict of the self. Today there is a tendency to believe that depression has to do with exhaustion – hence the coupling with another widespread diagnosis, stress. The fact that everything is possible, but that it isn't possible to do just anything, that people say yes all the time and expect enthusiasm while things come to nothing, that anything new is a grand idea, throws the individual into an exhaustive feeling of insufficiency. You can do anything and yet you can't do everything. If neurosis may be seen as an exposure of the drama of guilt, depression may be seen as the tragedy of insufficiency and exhaustion.

If the encounter with boundaries and the possibility of conflict are important for the creation of the self, it does not come as a surprise that the projectual individual may experience difficulties finding an identity and to sense itself. The Austrian writer Robert Musil made a characterisation of *The Man Without Qualities* at approximately the same time as Kafka sensed the faltering of judgement. His novel was a critique of modern times and a characterisation of modern man. The main character Ulrich is a person who knows a lot and is capable of doing a lot of things, but never gets to the bottom of anything, which is why he never manages to turn anything into a quality, everything just remains things he knows about or knows how to do. He lives in a world where there is no unifying world picture any longer. He lives in a society where there is no unifying idea anymore – there is but a project of celebrating the Kaiser.

In the project society the lack of a centre of the world and a centre of society has become the centre of a logic. And the individual project man and project woman go through their individual lives without any unifying life projects. A projectual life consists in overlapping projects and projections. Something came of something, a lot came to nothing, yet other things may never come to anything. If project people have great difficulties finding themselves as a consequence, it is no surprise that they take part in creating their profiles within a forum with such delight and ease – the putting together of an identity with invented qualities. We'll leave the project man there, in the balancing act, where it has difficulties at sensing itself, reaching out. Projecting. Perhaps it wouldn't be such an old-fashioned gesture after all to hand it a few limits or boundaries. But for the moment its eyes are wandering, in search for new openings.

References and Suggestions
for Further Reading

The Project Society is based on my book in Danish, *Projektsamfundet* (2009). In that book I offer a thorough account of the theoretical foundation of my theses and the various manifestations of the transition from disciplinary organisation to projectual life within ten different empirical areas: the social services, the combating of epidemics, ways of dancing, management, sports, football systems, coupling, architecture, education and warfare.

I mainly draw inspiration from the society I live in. Apart from that, Michel Foucault's ideas of disciplinary organisation, as unfolded in e.g. *Discipline and Punish* (1975) have played a great role. Ideas from this book are presented in chapter three in particular. Foucault's ideas of how power works through construction, activity and identity, and not only through oppression, have also been very relevant to me, e.g. as unfolded in *The History of Sexuality* (1976). In *The New Spirit of Capitalism* (1999) Luc Boltanski and Ève Chiapello explore the transformation of ways of legitimising capitalism and discuss the role of the project in the legitimisation of modern capitalism. I am inspired by their focus on work sociology, but I have tried to contemplate the project in a more philosophical perspective rather than limiting it to working conditions.

If you want precise references, exact data and elaborate

argumentation, I refer you to my book *Projektsamfundet*. The following is just an indication of the literature that has been most relevant to the line of thought within this book, apart from the books mentioned above.

In chapter one particularly Søren Kierkegaard's *The Illness and Death* (1849), Freidrich Nietzsche's *Beyond Good and Evil* (1886), Martin Heidegger's *Being and Time* (1927), Jean-Paul Sartre's *Being and Nothingness* (1943) form the basis of my delineation of the emergence of projectual man.

In chapter two I have used the *International Encyclopaedia of Dance* (1988) for the outline of the history of dance up until 1960 – aside from taking an extra look at the people around me at various parties.

Chapter four makes use of Gilles Deleuze and Félix Guattari's idea of territorialisation from *A Thousand Plateaus* (1980), N.J. Habraken's analysis of the relation between territory and form in *The Structure of the Ordinary* (1998). My ideas of the progress of pedagogics towards the development of individual skill rely on Jesper Juul's *Dit kompetente barn* (1998), flexibility in modern schools on Per Fibæk Laursen's *Den fleksible skole* (2006). Finally I have been watching a lot of football games, discussed them with my friends and read Niels Gunder Hansen and Frederik Stjernfelt's "Fodens kultivering og det stiliserede slag" in Christensen and Stjernfelt *Fodbold! Forfattere om fænomenet fodbold* (2002).

Chapter five takes its point of departure in Henri Bergson's ideas of time and duration, as offered in *Matière et mémoire*

(1910). For repetition, ethics and aesthetics, see Søren Kierkegaard's *Either/Or* (1843).

In chapter six I reproduce thoughts from Michel Foucault's "Des espaces autres" (1967) in analysis of the passage, and in the analysis of the social services from Niels Åkerstrøm Andersen's *Borgerens kontraktliggørelse* (2003).

Among other things, chapter seven includes the 94 episodes of the TV-series *Sex and the City* (Star & King 1998-2004). You can read about the organisation of armies (chapter eight) in Michael Hardt and Antonio Negri's *Multitude* (2004). You can read about the movements of globalisation in Naomi Klein's *No logo* (2000), among others.

You can also read more about flexibility and its human consequences, which are dealt with in chapter nine, in Richard Sennett's *The Corrosion of Character* (1998), although he approaches the topic from a rather nostalgic angle. For issues of formation and inconclusivity, read Gilles Deleuze's article, "Postscriptum sur les sociétés de contrôle" in *Pourparlers* (1990). Moreover, the condition of indeterminateness and its consequences for the self are displayed in Franz Kafka's *The Trial* (1925), Robert Musil's *The Man Without Qualities* (1930-33), Milan Kundera's *The Unbearable Lightness of Being* (1986), Michel Houellebecq's *The Elementary Particles* (1998) and Alain Ehrenberg's *La Fatigue d'être soi* (2000).

None of the works mentioned above have conceptualised society as a project society, even less man as a projectual being, which is why they cannot be called to account for the kind of distortion I have exposed their ideas to. Above all, this is a matter of borrowing concepts, inventing one or two yourself – and then set out to explore the world.